Test Process Improvement®

ACM PRESS BOOKS

This book is published as part of ACM Press Books – a collaboration between the Association for Computing (ACM) and Pearson Education Limited. ACM is the oldest and largest educational and scientific society in the information technology field. Through its high-quality publications and services, ACM is a major force in advancing the skills and knowledge of IT professionals throughout the world. For further information about ACM, contact:

ACM Member Services
1515 Broadway, 17th Floor
New York, NY 10036–5701
Phone: 1-212-626-0500
Fax: 1-212-944-1318
E-mail: acmhelp@acm.org

ACM European Service Center
108 Cowley Road
Oxford OX4 1JF
United Kingdom
Phone: +44-1865-382388
Fax: +44-1865-381388
E-mail: acm_europe@acm.org
URL: http://www.acm.org

Selected ACM titles

Component Software: Beyond Object-Oriented Programming *Clemens Szyperski*

The Object Advantage: Business Process Reengineering with Object Technology (2nd edn) *Ivar Jacobson, Maria Ericsson, Agneta Jacobson, Gunnar Magnusson*

Object-Oriented Software Engineering: A Use Case Driven Approach *Ivar Jacobson, Magnus Christerson, Patrik Jonsson, Gunnar Overgaard*

Software for Use: A Practical Guide to the Models and Methods of Usage Centered Design *Larry L Constantine, Lucy A D Lockwood*

Bringing Design to Software: Expanding Software Developments to Include Design *Terry Winograd, John Bennett, Laura de Young, Bradley Hartfield*

CORBA Distributed Objects: Using Orbix *Sean Baker*

Software Requirements and Specifications: A Lexicon of Software Practice, Principles and Prejudices *Michael Jackson*

Business Process Implementation: Building Workflow Systems *Michael Jackson, Graham Twaddle*

Interacting Processes: A Multiparty Approach to Coordinated Distributed Programming *Nissim Francez, Ira Forman*

Design Patterns for Object-Oriented Software Development *Wolfgang Pree*

Software Testing in the Real World: Improving the Process *Ed Kit*

Software Test Automation: Effective use of Test Execution Tools *Mark Fewster and Dorothy Graham*

Requirements Engineering and Rapid Development: An Object-Oriented Approach *Ian Graham*

Test Process Improvement®

*A practical step-by-step guide
to structured testing*

Tim Koomen
Martin Pol

An imprint of PEARSON EDUCATION

Harlow, England · London · New York · Reading, Massachusetts · San Francisco · Toronto · Don Mills, Ontario · Sydney
Tokyo · Singapore · Hong Kong · Seoul · Taipei · Cape Town · Madrid · Mexico City · Amsterdam · Munich · Paris · Milan

Pearson Education Limited

Head Office:
Edinburgh Gate
Harlow
Essex CM20 2JE
Tel: +44 (0) 1279 623623
Fax: +44 (0) 1279 431059

London Office:
128 Long Acre
London WC2E 9AN
Tel: +44 (0)20 7447 2000
Fax: +44 (0)20 7240 5771

and Associated Companies throughout the world

Visit us on the world wide web at:
http://www.awl.com/cseng

First published in Great Britain 1999

ISBN 0-201-59624-5

British Library Cataloguing-in-Publication Data
A catalogue record for this book is available from the British Library.

10 9 8 7 6 5 4 3

Typeset by CRB Associates, Norfolk.
Printed and bound by Biddles Ltd, Guildford and King's Lynn.
Cover designed by OdB Design and Communication, Reading, UK
and printed by The Riverside Printing Co. (Reading) Ltd.

The publishers' policy is to use paper manufactured from sustainable forests.

Foreword

by Henk W. Broeders, CAP Gemini NV

Those readers who have been working in IT for a long period of time will remember the days when testing was the task of the most junior person on the team. Since then, testing has come a long way – to the point where it is recognized now as a real profession. Testing indeed has developed into a specialization, and not because the most junior person on the team gained seniority. With the growing complexity of IT systems, the need for more thorough testing became evident. The overall goal of testing became not just to identify errors in a single program, but to validate the correct functioning of a large number of integrated IT components.

This wider challenge could no longer be faced with the techniques the junior programmer had available, and more sophisticated testing techniques and approaches developed over the years. IQUIP's method TMap is an excellent example of these.

Now we are at a third stage. The importance of IT has grown dramatically: IT is no longer just a tool for efficiency improvement, but has become the key to new markets and improved competitiveness. It will add more and more to the effectiveness of organizations.

Organizations all over the world are searching for the best IT solutions in their marketplace. And very often they find the answer in complex sets of packaged applications. Packages that are supplemented with unique bespoke software are the core of competitive advantage creation for many organizations. It is my conviction that these sets of applications will come from various sources – that multiple vendors will provide a blend of tailor made software and existing packages to the corporate consumer. The complexity of software integration will grow very rapidly, and as the need for robustness of these systems will not diminish, testing will become more important. And its importance will continue to grow.

The practice-based Test Process Improvement model will prove to be the key to robustness and to the use of the complex systems that are needed to deal with the changed role of IT in business.

In other words, if competitiveness is an issue in your market, IT will be vital, and this book will help you to deal with the problems it will bring along.

Henk W. Broeders
Member of the Executive Board of CAP Gemini NV
President of Fenit – the Federation of Dutch IT companies
Utrecht, January 1999

Foreword

by Dr Hans Voorthuyzen, Baan Company

Once upon a time, in an earlier era of software engineering, it was possible that after a long period of designing and coding, a short, ad-hoc test would be organized to assess and validate a final product, just prior to its launch to the market.

Today, more and more people are involved professionally in the fascinating field of testing. New IT products flood the marketplace at an unexpectedly high and still increasing frequency, and as a consequence, no modern software engineering organization with any degree of self-esteem can continue to follow the mythical approach of ad-hoc and unprepared testing.

What is more, the intelligence and complexity of new software products is booming. So creating a professional testing regime, which is fully embedded in the product development cycle and synchronized with all related processes, has become a must. This may seem obvious to the reader, but many organizations are still working on the basics of testing. Is it not remarkable that this year only the sixth European conference on software testing, EuroSTAR, will be organized, while Software Engineering Conferences have a much longer and older tradition?

Learning from one another is a self-evident characteristic of the young discipline of software testing. Unfortunately, most of the knowledge and experience is not, however, available explicitly. For that reason it was a pleasure to learn several months ago that the research and development department of Software Control Testen (a specialized testing department of IQUIP Informatica B.V.) was working on a new initiative, TPI: Test Process Improvement.

I am very proud to be able to say that before TPI was launched officially and presented to the press, Baan Development was allowed to run a pilot. I am also glad to state here that TPI has been 'tested' by our Product Testing

Group on locations in India, USA and the Netherlands, and that we could give TPI the green light.

The application of TPI in our 100-plus sized department enables us to raise our global testing organization to the next professional level. I am absolutely convinced that everybody using TPI in a similar way will experience the same added value.

Finally, I congratulate IQUIP with the presentation of TPI.

Dr Hans Voorthuyzen
Global Manager Product Testing Group
Baan Development, Baan Company
Barneveld, August 1998

Foreword

by Stephen K. Allott, Imago^{QA} *Limited*

Many companies recognize the need to improve the quality of their testing effort. Reduced development timeframes and increasing application complexity have highlighted poor quality testing in many organizations. Test and QA departments are being stretched as never before. Improving time to market due to competitive pressures has never been more important but the customer, quite rightly, still expects a high quality product.

Often the first thing that companies do to solve the problem is to buy an automated testing tool. Why not? – after all, that's what I did, twice, and it didn't help as much as I had expected.

When I was responsible for performance and stress testing for a major UK Bank some years ago we tried to introduce the latest automated testing tools. Trying to develop a new test process for the QA and testing department to help them use the new tools proved more difficult than I imagined, but I did not know why at the time. Implementation of the tool was only partially successful.

More recently, as a test manager for a small yet growing software house, I again tried to introduce improvements to the test process. This time I focused on test planning and test techniques. However, I still believed that test automation was the way forward, especially with the ever increasing number of databases and operating systems in use by the customers of the products. Developing a new test process and trying to introduce test automation proved time consuming and difficult, and again I could not understand the reason.

Finally, at a testing conference in 1997, I was introduced to TPI and suddenly the penny dropped. As soon as I got back to the office I quickly answered all of the questions in the TPI model. This was quite a revelation. When I joined the company, a year earlier, the key areas of Test tools and

Key area	Scale													
	0	1	2	3	4	5	6	7	8	9	10	11	12	13
Test strategy		A					B				C		D	
Life-cycle model		A			B									
Moment of involvement			A				B				C		D	
Estimating and planning				A							B			
Test specification techniques		A		B										
Static test techniques					A		B							
Metrics						A			B			C		D
Test tools					A			B		C				
Test environment				A				B						C
Office environment				A										
Commitment and motivation		A				B						C		
Test functions and training				A			B			C				
Scope of methodology					A						B			C
Communication			A		B							C		
Reporting		A			B		C					D		
Defect management		A				B		C						
Testware management			A			B				C				D
Test process management		A		B								C		
Evaluation							A			B				
Low-level testing					A		B		C					

Moment of involvement were well established (both at level A on the TPI matrix), as was Reporting and Defect management. But none of the other key areas had been given any attention. By the end of 1997 we had the situation shown in the above table.

I began to understand that a test manager has to give attention to several of the key areas at once. Following this analysis carried out with the help of the TPI model, we focused our next attention on:

- **Test environment** We built a test lab with several servers, PCs, modems etc.;

- **Communication** We held regular weekly meetings involving both testers and developers;

- **Metrics** We maintained and published weekly numbers of bugs, out-standing time to fix and so on.

Another useful aspect of the TPI method is its visual impact on senior management. You can prepare a simple, one-page chart every 3 months, say, with the key areas highlighted. They can easily see your progress throughout the year on how you are improving your test process. And when asked why you need more office space for example, or why you need to buy a testware management tool, you can drill down into the detailed questions and explain the reasons with increased confidence.

I recommend that you try the ideas suggested in this book. Try not to get bogged down by interpreting the questions too literally. If you need to add a question, or reword one to fit your particular environment, then by all means do so but please feed back your experiences to the authors. And do not try to tell your management that you are at a particular level; simply show them the diagram and explain where you are with each of your key areas. Please use the TPI method to improve your test process. And when you're successful, why not present a paper at a testing conference and share your success with the testing community?

Stephen K. Allott BSc(Hons) MBCS
Programme Secretary
BCS Specialist Interest Group in Software Testing (SIGIST)
Senior Consultant, Imago^{QA} Limited
Chelmsford, January 1999

Acknowledgments

It goes without saying that the development of the TPI model and this book would not have been possible without the input of a large number of co-workers. In view of the importance we attach to this input, we would like to thank the following people:

Rob Baarda, Bart Broekman, Klaas Brongers, Wieger van Brug, Mark Buenen, Rob Dekker, Bart Ellen, Ed van der Geest, Henk Grondel, Bart Hendriks, Christiaan Hoos, Kees Hopman, Rob Kuijt, Frank Langeveld, Bert Noorman, Mark Paap, Désirée Pardoel, André van Pelt, Marjolein Steyerberg, Gerrit de Vries, members of the initial expertise group: Frank Geerts, Joost van Haarlem, Henk Jacobs, and Corné de Koning, all from IQUIP, and Han Gerritsen of ING Barings and Stefan Steurs of Eurocontrol – CFMU in Belgium.

We are also very grateful to Steve Allott of Imago^{QA} Limited, Gregory Daich of the Software Technology Support Centre and Jos van Rooyen of Baan Development for reviewing an early draft of this book and for making numerous invaluable remarks.

Finally, we thank Ingrid Ottevanger for her patience and ceaseless effort in bringing together reviewers, editors, publishers and (sometimes difficult) authors.

Contents

Trademark notice
Microsoft Excel is a trademark of Microsoft Corporation; TAKT, TPI, and
TSite are trademarks or registered trademarks of Software Control Testen;
TMap is a trademark or registered trademark of IQUIP Informatica B.V.

CHAPTER ONE

Introduction

Testing is a must! Testing is a necessary prerequisite for successfully building and implementing information technology (IT) systems. But often testing is regarded as a necessary evil: it is looked upon as a difficult and uncontrollable process, which takes too much time and money and will usually not result in an IT system that can be implemented without any problems.

Unfortunately, in many cases this opinion is justified. Although testing accounts for between 25 and 50% of the total project budget, in only a few organizations does management spend the appropriate amount of time needed to manage such a large sub-process in the correct manner.

Structuring the test process can solve many of the problems related to testing. Structured testing means that a (documented) set of activities, procedures, and techniques is used, covering all aspects of the test process. In practice, however, it seems to be difficult to determine which steps have to be taken in which order to improve this process.

1.1 The TPI model

For controlled and gradual improvement of testing, we have defined a Test Process Improvement (TPI) model, based on the knowledge and experience of the company IQUIP. The TPI model offers a frame of reference for determining the strong and weak points of an organization's current test process. Also, the model supports the setting up of specific and realistic proposals for the improvement of this test process in terms of lead time, costs, and quality. The model is based on the structured test approach TMap (Pol *et al.*, 1995) but can be used in almost any test process.

This book contains a comprehensive description of the TPI model and also deals with the use of the model in improving the test process. The model emerged from practice and experience, and scientific proof of the validity of the model is not supplied. The model is published so that it can be used and therefore evolve as a result. The authors want to serve as intermediaries in describing this initial version, but also in the improvement of the model, the 'TPI improvement process.' For this reason, an Internet communication channel has been opened: http://www.iquip.nl/tpi (see Appendix A; information is available in English, German and Dutch).

1.2 How this book is structured

The book is structured as follows:

- Chapter 2 describes the overall scope of testing.

- Chapter 3 deals with the necessity of improving the test process.

- Chapter 4 indicates why a model is needed for this.

- Chapter 5 gives an overall description of the TPI model: key areas with levels, the Test Maturity Matrix, and checkpoints and improvement suggestions for each level.

- Chapter 6 deals with the change process for improving the testing process and explains how the model can be employed within such a process.

- Chapter 7 is primarily a reference chapter. The levels of each key area, together with the related checkpoints and improvement suggestions, are described.

- The appendices contain a summary of TMap, a brief overview of the categories of test tools and some points of interest for the use of test tools.

1.3 Who this book is for

This book is written for people who are involved in some way in the testing of information technology (IT) systems and, more specifically, in the improvement of the test process (as customer or as executor). Readers are expected to have an overall knowledge of testing within the IT business, without having to possess specific knowledge of a test methodology. Therefore, the first chapter dealing with the concepts of testing is relatively short. For those who wish to read more about these concepts, there is plenty of reference material. People like Beizer, Hetzel, Kit and Pol/Van Veenendaal have written excellent books on the subject (Beizer, 1990; Hetzel, 1993; Kit, 1995; Pol and Van Veenendaal, 1998).

Readers who intend to be active in improving the test process are recommended to study Chapters 3 to 7 thoroughly. For those who are considering improving the test process, commissioning this improvement, or who are only partially involved in the improvement process, studying Chapters 3 to 6 is sufficient. Depending on readers' prior knowledge of testing, or to familiarize themselves with some of the terms used in the book, it can be useful to read Chapter 2. Those who are only interested in an overall description of the model can confine themselves to reading Chapter 5.

1.4 How the TPI model developed

The model was developed because IQUIP and its customers had an increasing need for a model that supported improvements to a test process. For this reason, an expertise group was founded in 1996 to investigate which models were usable. Several existing models were examined and their pros and cons discussed. No single model turned out to have the various qualities required. This outcome led to the definition of the outline of a new model, the TPI model, in 1997. Although many minor adjustments have been made to the model in the course of time, the original outline has not been changed. During the remainder of 1997 the model was elaborated further and put into practice. Also, we decided to publish the model as a book. The Dutch book was written in 1997; in the first part of 1998, several presentations were given and the model was put into further use. This English translation was done in the second part of 1998. A German edition is due later in 1999.

Diemen, January 1999
Tim Koomen
Martin Pol

CHAPTER TWO

The scope of testing

In this chapter we explain a number of concepts and frames of reference. We describe what testing actually is, why we do it and which products we can expect a test process to deliver. We compare testing with evaluation and place it in the scope of quality assurance. The last two sections deal with the concepts of test levels and their relationship to the development process. As this book is primarily focused on (a model for) test process improvement and assumes that readers are familiar with the concept of testing, this chapter is relatively short.

2.1 What is testing?

Testing always involves comparison; it requires a test object and a frame of reference with which that object should comply, a test basis. Testing gives insight into the difference between the actual and the required status of an object.

Many definitions of the concept of testing are available. TMap (Pol *et al.*, 1995) provides a manageable definition of the concept of 'testing' within the scope of administrative automation. We will use this definition in this book:

Testing is a process of planning, preparation, and measuring aimed at establishing the characteristics of an information system and demonstrating the difference between the actual and the required status.

Specifically, the inclusion of activities such as planning and preparation emphasizes the fact that testing should not be regarded as a process that only begins when the object to be tested is delivered. A test process requires good planning and preparation before the actual 'measurement' can be done.

2.2 Purpose of testing

In developing and maintaining information systems, special attention should be paid to quality. In this case, quality is the fulfilling of the expectations of different users. In practice this is a delicate matter for the IT business; only a few branches of industry suffer from such a poor quality image. Quality refers to reliability, to delivery in time and within budget, and to meeting the initial target, which is to offer a solution to a problem.

With quality roughly defined as 'meeting requirements,' testing gives insight into the quality level. In this way it clearly shows the risks which are taken when accepting a lower quality. This leads to the main objective of testing:

Testing reduces the level of uncertainty about the quality of an IT system.

Testing, however, costs time and money. The test customer has to decide how much time and money is to be spent on reducing the level of uncertainty. The level of the testing effort depends on the risks involved in bringing the IT system into operation.

No risk, no test

Testing is based on a best possible spot-check of all possible situations that can arise within the IT system; in practice this is never exhaustive. It is of the greatest importance to understand that testing shows only symptoms. This causes a considerable danger that testing merely leads to the treatment of symptoms; only the defects that are found are corrected.

However, the result of testing should lead to making a diagnosis; that is, detecting the causes *behind* the problems. A diagnosis is not based on an isolated complaint, but on the recognition of a pattern in the complaints. Based on the diagnosis, the recovery process can be started. In the case of IT systems this means much more than solving an isolated problem. *Structural quality enhancement should start top-down.* Quality must be *built*, not *tested*, into a system! One of the building blocks of quality thinking is that prevention is better (and importantly, cheaper) than cure. Prevention is part of the preliminary path in system development. Quality improvement by means of testing is extremely expensive. Based on this principle, the testing of a bad system should be stopped and redevelopment should be started.

The observed symptoms enable an organization to make a diagnosis and to solve problems. But, equally important, these symptoms offer an opportunity to say something about the risks involved in taking a certain version of the software into operation. Based on the symptoms seen during testing, a prediction can be made, by means of extrapolation, of the behavior of the system in a production environment. This estimate is of vital importance for the persons responsible for the delivery or acceptance of the system. Many problems can be prevented if, as a result of good risk analysis, the conclusion is reached that successful implementation of a release cannot be done, or can only partially be done. Postponing the implementation of a system is painful and often very expensive. Implementing a bad system, however, is much more expensive and also much more painful.

2.3 Products

The most important products of a test process are:

- Detected defects. The differences between the expectations and the actual results are called **defects**. These defects and how they are dealt with should be carefully documented.
- Information and advice about the quality of the test object. Based on, in the first instance, the defects found, the test process gives the customer insight into the quality of the tested system and provides release advice for the next phase. The term 'advice' is emphasized here, because testers have no decision authorization. The customer can still, in spite of negative release advice, decide to take the system into production. A possible reason for this is that the costs involved in not meeting a deadline can be several times higher than the possible costs of insufficient system quality.
- Testware. In the testing process, test plans are made, test cases specified, test databases and files set up, test output created, and so on. These products are called **testware**. It is important to regard this testware not as a disposable product, but as one that has to be filed, managed, and handed over for reuse upon test completion. A result of this is that in later tests, and also in the maintenance phase, time-consuming preparation activities can be avoided.
- Other test documentation. Besides the testware, several other documents are produced, such as accounts and reports.

- Indicators. During testing, figures are collected concerning the progress, size, and quality of the test process. These figures can be translated into indicators that form valuable control data for further test processes.

Note that the tested IT system itself is not recognized as a test product, because the test process adds nothing to, and adjusts nothing in, the IT system.

2.4 The role of testing within quality management

As mentioned earlier, delivering quality products is still a problem in the IT industry. Testing is not a solution for this. Testing is just one instrument that can contribute to the quality enhancement of IT systems. Testing should be embedded in a system of measures to reach a certain quality level: testing should be embedded in the *quality management* of an organization.

In the formulation of a theory about quality management, a number of concepts have been developed. ISO, the International Standards Organization, has played an important role in achieving uniform definitions. According to ISO the definition of quality is:

The totality of features and characteristics of a product or a service that bear on its ability to satisfy stated or implied needs. (ISO 8402)

This definition clearly has 'elusive' aspects. What is implied or obvious to one person is not obvious at all to another. Implicitness and obviousness are pre-eminently subjective notions. Therefore, an important aspect of quality management is minimizing the implied needs, by converting these into requirements and making visible the extent to which these requirements are met.

For that purpose, measures are taken to determine these requirements and to make the development process manageable. These measures can be described as 'quality assurance':

All planned and systematic actions necessary to provide adequate confidence that a product or service will satisfy given requirements for quality. (ISO 8402)

These actions can be divided into preventive, detective, and corrective measures:

- Preventive measures aim to *prevent* lack of quality. For example, documentation norms, methods, techniques, and so on.

- Detective measures aim to *discover* lack of quality. For example, conducting reviews, walkthroughs, and, of course, testing.

- Corrective measures aim to *remedy* lack of quality, such as correcting defects discovered by testing.

These measures should lead to:

- measuring points and entities which indicate process quality (setting the standard);

- clarity for individual employees as to which standards their work should meet and the ability for them to check it by using the norms mentioned above;

- the possibility for an independent party to test the products/services by using the norms mentioned above;

- the ability for management to trace defects found in products and to prevent these defects from occurring in the future.

It is of vital importance that there is a connection between the individual measures. Testing is not a standalone activity. Testing is merely a building block in the quality management structure; it is one of the forms of quality detection that can be used. In turn, quality detection is merely one of the activities to assure quality. Finally, quality assurance is only one of the dimensions of quality management.

Taking measures in the scope of quality management costs money. Lack of quality (management) also costs money: the costs of failure. The total of these different kinds of costs is called **quality costs**. Figure 2.1, taken from Juran (1988), displays the relationship between the different kinds of costs.

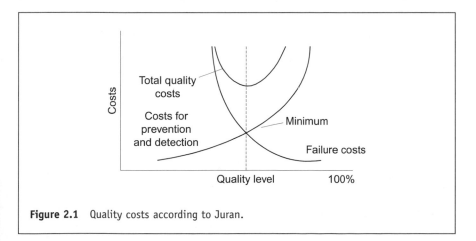

Figure 2.1   Quality costs according to Juran.

The figure shows that there is a minimum in the total quality costs. Quality costs are:

- **prevention costs**   costs of taking preventive measures;

- **detection costs**   costs of taking detective measures;

- **failure costs**   costs of taking corrective measures, or costs as a result of insufficient quality (lost income, extra service costs, guarantee claims, damage claims).

An important message Juran gives us is that pursuing perfect quality is not cost-effective, because eventually each small increase in quality will require a large investment. Freely translated for testing, this message is:

Testing should continue as long as the costs of finding and correcting a defect are lower than the costs of failure in operation.

2.5 Testing and evaluation

Testing belongs to the detective measures of a quality system. It is related to reviewing, simulation, inspection, auditing, sampling, desk-checking, walkthroughs, and so on. The various detection instruments are divided into two groups: evaluation and testing.

Evaluation, often also called verification, means examining intermediate products of the development phases, mostly by inspecting or reviewing documents. **Did we build well?** Evaluation normally does not involve executing software. **Testing**, or validation, means inspecting the end product, and is done by executing software. Is the product valid in relation to the requirements? **Did we build the right product?** The separation between evaluation and testing is not a black and white one. For instance, an

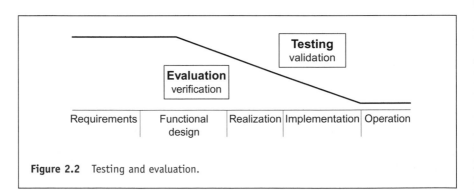

Figure 2.2   Testing and evaluation.

important aspect in the preparation of testing is evaluation of the test basis to see if it is sufficiently testable. Evaluation, for example, also implies inspecting the testware (see Figure 2.2).

2.6 Test levels and techniques

To gain insight into the actual and the required status of an IT system, it is important to realize that there is no one specific document which contains the required status. There are, for instance, user and technical requirements; based on these requirements a functional design is specified, followed by a technical design and the actual coding of the software. It is not sufficient for insight into the system quality to test only whether the software works according to the functional or technical design, because this design can be flawed. Neither is it sufficient to test only whether the software works according to user requirements, because these are at such an abstract level that the derived test cases do not cover enough of the software code or even enough of the total system functionality to gain sufficient insight into the quality. The answer, of course, is that all kinds of tests need to be employed, based on different requirements. Tests are needed to validate whether the program works according to the technical design, whether the application works according to the functional design, and whether the system fulfills the users' needs and wishes.

To organize these tests efficiently, different test levels are used, where each test level addresses a certain group of requirements or functional or technical specifications.

A test level is a group of test activities that are organized and directed collectively.

Examples of test levels are the unit test, integration test, system test, and acceptance test.

Based on the assigned requirements and the risks involved if the requirements are not met, each test level defines a test strategy to find the most important errors as early and as efficiently as possible. In more mature organizations these different test level strategies are closely co-ordinated by means of a master test plan, resulting in an optimized overall test strategy.

An important aspect in the definition of the strategy is the choice of which test specification techniques to use. These techniques are a structured approach to deriving test cases from the test basis (for instance, requirements, functional, or technical specifications) and are aimed at detecting certain kinds of defects. The use of well-chosen techniques results in far more effective detection of defects than random identification of test cases.

To measure how thoroughly tested a product is, the term **coverage** of a test can be used: the ratio between that which can be tested (possible number of test aims) and that which is in fact tested. Coverage is often used in relation to program code ('with the available test cases X% of all statements or conditions is covered') but is also possible in relation to the functional specifications or requirements (paths, conditions, or interfaces).

The test specification techniques can be split into two groups: white-box and black-box techniques. **White-box** testing techniques are based on the program code, the program descriptions, or the technical design. Knowledge of the internal structure of the system plays an important role. **Black-box** testing techniques are based on the functional specifications and quality requirements. In black-box techniques the system is viewed as it will be in actual use. In theory, knowledge about the structure of the system is not used. Judgment is made merely from a functional point of view of the system. Only the outside matters. Does the 'black box' indeed deliver output B from input A, in time frame C, in environment D, and so on?

The test levels can be grouped into two categories that are of importance in the context of this book: low-level tests and high-level tests.

2.6.1 Low-level tests

These test levels involve testing the separate components of a system, for instance programs, individually or in combination (Kit, 1995). The tests are almost exclusively executed by developers.

From the very beginning of the first building blocks of the system, *unit, program, and module tests* are executed. The extent to which separate tests for units, programs, or modules are done depends on the infrastructure and programming language used. It is necessary to check that the most elementary parts or collections of parts are coded in accordance with the technical specifications. This book exclusively uses the term *unit test* with regard to this subject.

A **unit test** is a test, executed by the developer in a laboratory environment, that should demonstrate that the program meets the requirements set in the design specifications.

After it has been determined that the most elementary parts of the system are of good quality, larger parts of the system are tested as a whole during the integration tests. The emphasis is on data throughput and the interface between the programs at a system part level. The integration test represents, so to speak, an assembly test. Depending on the development strategy, the system will be delivered step by step and tested integrally with an increasing number of parts.

An **integration test** is a test, executed by the developer in a laboratory environment, that should demonstrate that a logical series of programs meets the requirements set in the design specifications.

As the low-level tests require good knowledge of the internal structure of the software, mainly white-box testing techniques are applicable.

2.6.2 High-level tests

These tests involve testing whole, complete products (Kit, 1995).

High-level tests offer the developer insight into the quality of the system offered for acceptance. Also, the tests inform the customer, user, and manager about the extent to which the requirements are met and the system can (again) be taken into production. After the low-level tests have been executed and the defects found have been corrected, the developer executes a *system test* to determine whether the system meets the functional and technical design specifications. In practice this means in general that parts of the system are tested 'tile-wise' until the whole system can be tested integrally. The system test requires a controllable environment with regard to the application and test data.

A **system test** is a test, executed by the developer or independent test team in a (properly controllable) laboratory environment, that should demonstrate that the developed system or subsystems meet the requirements set in the functional and quality specifications.

After the developer has performed the system test and has corrected the defects encountered, the system will be offered to the customer for acceptance. Then the specified acceptance tests can be performed. The *acceptance test* should answer questions such as: Can the system (again) be taken into production and maintenance? What risks am I taking when I do this? Has the supplier met his or her obligations? The execution of the acceptance test requires an environment that is, in most respects, representative of the production environment ('as-if-production').

An **acceptance test** is a test, executed by the user(s) and system manager(s) in an environment simulating the operational environment to the greatest possible extent, that should demonstrate that the developed system meets the functional and quality requirements.

Within the acceptance test, two test levels can be recognized which, because of their special character, are usually prepared and executed separately. The functional acceptance test focuses mainly on the functionality and suitability, while the production acceptance test validates whether the system meets the requirements for operation. The functional acceptance test is performed by the users and functional managers and, in terms of planning, is usually linked tightly to the system test; it will, in many cases, be organized 'tile-wise' at the start. The production acceptance test will, in most cases, be performed by the system managers shortly before the system is taken into production.

The high-level tests especially can be regarded as individual processes (and can therefore be organized as such). These are processes, parallel to the development process, which start during the Functional Design phase. Good management of these processes and tuning in with the rest of the project by means of reporting and communication are vital. Past experience has shown that awareness of the importance of a good test process is greater with high-level tests than with low-level tests.

As their focus is often the externally visible properties of an object, high-level tests commonly use black-box techniques. However, the line between low-level/white-box and high-level/black-box tests is not as 'black and white' as it seems. High-level tests increasingly appear to require knowledge of the internal operation and structure of the system. On the other hand, typical low-level tests, such as unit tests, increasingly use functional specifications as a test basis.

2.7 Relationship between the development and test processes

The development of IT systems is in most cases still done by the most current life-cycle model, the waterfall method:

1   starting, company-wide, to define the possibilities offered by the IT technology for the solution of problems or the optimization of the business processes and the assignment of priorities (information policy, information planning);

2   determining roughly *which functional and non-functional requirements* the system should meet (information analysis, definition study);

3   determining *which* functionality should be developed (functional design);

4   determining *how* this should be solved (technical design);

5   creating the system and subsequently testing, implementing, and using it.

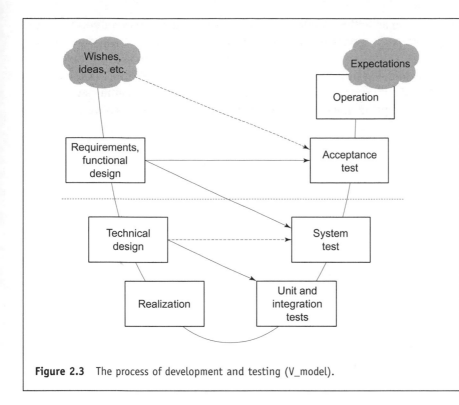

Figure 2.3 The process of development and testing (V_model).

The terminology used above originates from *a* life-cycle model. There are numerous life-cycle models. They all share, in one way or another, a similar approach. This also applies to modern variations on the classic model, for example Rapid Application Development (RAD) and Evolutionary Development.

The variety in test levels can be well related to such a life-cycle model.

A widely employed presentation of the life-cycle model for system development and testing is the V_model (see Figure 2.3).

On the left side of the model are the phases in which the system is built or rebuilt, from wish, idea, need, law, policy, change, and/or requirement to solution. On the right side is test execution. The dotted line (formally) shows the formal separation of responsibilities between customer, user, system manager, and computer center (above the line) and system developer, supplier, and programmer. For testing especially, it is very important to determine responsibilities. Who commissions a test? Who wants a quality report? Against each development phase there are one or more test levels.

The blocks of the V_model only represent the execution phases of the different test levels. The execution phase forms only 40% of the total effort of such a test level. The arrows represent the path of the base documentation (the test basis) to the execution of the test, the (60%) planning and preparation activities. The V_model makes clear that the execution phases of the various test levels are located on the critical path of the development process: they form, so to speak, the intersection between the test process and the development process. It goes without saying that it is important to round off the planning and preparation activities before the actual start of test execution, during quiet periods for the tester while the software developers are busy.

CHAPTER THREE

Need for improvement

This book aims at improving the test process. First, we should ask ourselves why we want to improve it. Section 3.1 outlines a number of situations showing that organizations encounter various problems with testing. Testing is generally experienced as expensive and time-consuming, while the tested systems do not have the expected quality level. If no measures are taken, these problems will increase in the future, rather than decrease. The next section shows that improving the test process is a solution for this.

3.1 Problems concerning testing

3.1.1 Primitive testing

Although much has been written about how testing should ideally take place, it turns out that daily practice is far removed from this. A 'primitive' form of testing which is still seen regularly is that an activity 'Testing' is started shortly before a system goes back into production. In the very limited time remaining, testing is performed by someone who is 'accidentally' available. The test cases are mostly suitable for one-time use by the tester himself and there is no insight into the level of completeness or thoroughness of the test. The activity usually stops at the moment when a system goes back into production, or when no defects have been found for some time. The result of this procedure is often that the system is accepted with many defects still remaining. This lack of quality results in expensive and almost permanently ongoing rework and retest activities.

3.1.2 Current state of affairs

Having learned the hard way, recognizing the importance of a well-managed test process is much more common nowadays. Tests are planned and prepared before the actual execution takes place. Test cases are based on, among other things, functional specifications, so that there is some insight into what has and what has not been tested. Although this is quite a step in the right direction, in many organizations the test process still cannot be controlled very well. Testing is usually short of time, people, resources, and expertise. Testing is involved late in the development cycle and often leads to a seemingly endless and very expensive cycle of rework, retest, rework, retest, and so on. Finally, when the testing stops, it is still uncertain whether the testing has given enough insight into the quality of the test object. When an attempt is made to make the test process faster and/or cheaper by applying tools, it often appears that the opposite result is achieved. Also, the testware is insufficiently reusable, so that much time is lost in re-creating the necessary testware.

By the way, the test process cannot be held solely responsible for high corrective costs or long project duration; a poor development process also plays a part. Testing merely establishes the fact that the quality of the system is insufficient. Much effort is subsequently needed to improve this quality. What testing can do, increasingly, is to point out (lack of) quality and to ensure that tests can be performed as cheaply and as quickly as possible.

3.1.3 New developments

Although the current state of affairs cannot be called entirely satisfactory, all kinds of new developments are dawning that might provide an extra challenge for the test process. To be able to face the competition in the current market, an organization must continue to shorten the time-to-market for new products. Supportive IT systems often form an important part of these new products. As a result, pressure from within the organization to shorten the time required to bring new or adapted systems into production increases (Boreel, Franken, 1997). Also, IT systems are increasingly used for customer communication, and the integration of different IT systems is becoming more important. An example is Internet applications or Computer Telephone Integration systems, which are in their turn linked, for example, to ordering and invoicing systems. This results in operational management being increasingly dependent on IT systems that have high-quality functioning. The negative consequences of insufficient quality in a system will therefore become more profound. Customers will become less inclined to accept the answer 'It is not our fault, the computer is down.'

Finally, IT innovations play an important role. The introduction of Rapid Application Development (RAD), graphical user interfaces, object

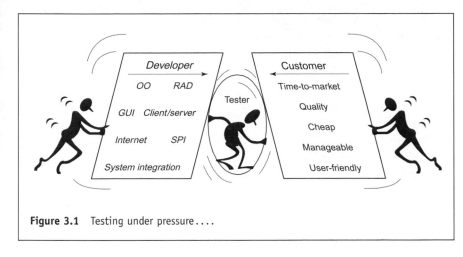

Figure 3.1 Testing under pressure....

orientation, and architectures such as Client/Server may cause the development process to speed up in what is, from a technical point of view, a heterogeneous environment. Although the process goes faster, there is no reason to suppose this will decrease the number of errors that are made in a certain period of time. Lack of experience and increased technical complexity justify the proposition that the number of errors made in a certain period of time stays at least the same (Beizer, 1990). An example of increased complexity is the almost unlimited number of processing combinations in a graphically oriented user interface compared with the far more restricted number of combinations in a character-oriented user interface. Yet in general it is regarded as unacceptable that the profit in the form of shorter project development time is used to extend the test process.

The conclusion of the above discussion is that even if the test process is reasonably satisfying for the current situation, this will not be the case for the future (see Figure 3.1).

3.2 Improving the test process

The cause of many of the problems mentioned above can be traced to an uncontrolled or badly arranged test process. It is obvious that this process should be improved. Because everyone has his or her own notion of test process improvement, it is a good idea to dwell upon the definition of test process improvement as it is employed in this book:

'Optimizing the quality, costs, and lead time of the test process, in relation to the total information services'

'Quality' stands for the degree of insight given by the test process concerning the quality of the tested object. A larger degree of insight can, for example, be obtained by more thorough testing, but also by means of better reporting. An important note is that the quality of the system or program is not part of this definition: the natural result of a qualitatively improved test process is not better quality of the tested system. Testing itself does not add quality to the system; it can merely determine the available quality and make it possible for others (designers, developers) to improve the quality using this information.

'In relation to the total information services' means that the test process is not on its own. Faster, cheaper, or better testing should not be a goal in itself; it should contribute to better performance of the total information services. Obviously, it is not efficient to do a very thorough, time-consuming test on a system that is used for membership administration of the local soccer team. On the other hand, it is useless to do a quick and cheap test after which undetected defects cause a major failure in a system and end up on the front pages of the national newspapers.

3.2.1 Scope of the test process improvement

The test process is a part of the total development process. In analyzing the problems concerning testing it is of the utmost importance to distinguish between the test process itself and the activities that have an impact on the test process. These activities (for example, functional design or realization) are not a subject of test process improvement.

The following examples try to explain how difficult it is to make this distinction:

- **Quality of the system** When a system often breaks down in production or when the product does not meet users' expectations, can you blame the testers?
  - Yes, because they have tested badly.
  - No, because the expectations were unclear.
  - No, because the users have not been prepared and trained well enough.
  - No, because the project organization took a conscious risk to do a limited test on last-minute changes and, despite negative release advice from the testers, to take the system into production anyway.

- **Time** The test paths are lengthy and often exceed the time allowed in the plan. As a result, a shorter time-to-market for the systems to be delivered cannot be achieved. Can you blame the testers for this?
  - Yes, because testing starts much too late and is not performed efficiently enough.

    – No, because the lack of quality of the systems to be delivered causes a need for extensive retesting.

- **Money** Although the quality of the delivered systems is found to be satisfactory, there are a large number of people involved in testing; can you blame the testers for this?
  - Yes, because the test team always carries out very thorough and labor-intensive tests.
  - No, because the extensive testing is regarded by other parties as a reason to put less effort into assuring good quality. It has been found on several occasions that developers had not tested their programs.

A restriction in improving only the test process is that efficiency decreases if the rest of the development process does not catch up with this process.

For example, testing shows that the quality of the software is insufficient. This leads to repair of the software and the next delivery for testing. This delivery is tested again and once again the software is diagnosed to be of insufficient quality. When this becomes a time-consuming cycle of reworking, retesting, and again diagnosing insufficient quality, the total process is far from being optimal. A good test process spots this trend, for instance by analysis of detected defects, and is able to give advice, but test process improvement does not deal with the improvement of the other development processes. Tools are available for improving the total development process (Software Process Improvement), such as the Capability Maturity Model (Humphrey, 1989; SEI, 1995), Bootstrap (Kuvaja *et al.*, 1994), and others.

In any case, improvement of the software development process is only one of a much larger group of aspects that influence the total results of system development (see also Figure 3.2).

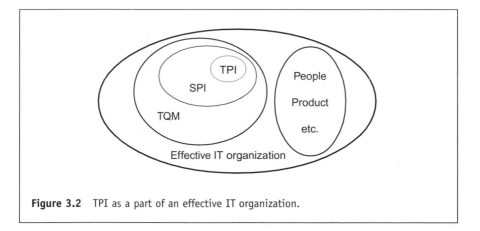

Figure 3.2 TPI as a part of an effective IT organization.

3.2.2 An improved test process

What can we think of in terms of an improved test process? To improve the test process in the long term, a number of solutions can be given.

As shown in Boehm (1979), the costs of correction increase exponentially throughout the system development phases. Figure 3.3 shows the correction costs in comparison to the phase in which the defect is found. The main point of the evaluation and test effort should therefore be brought forward in comparison to the development process. The aim should be to detect defects as close as possible to their source of injection, to minimize correction costs, and to give advice about system quality as early as possible. This implies a shift in the total evaluation and test effort from high-level tests towards earlier detection activities like evaluation and low-level tests. It also implies that all evaluation and test levels should be carefully adjusted to each other to achieve an optimized total strategy for detecting the most important defects as early and as cheaply as possible. The different test levels use different test specification techniques, each technique aimed at finding certain kinds of defects.

Furthermore, the testing should become more preventive in nature; in other words, the aim of testing should be that as few mistakes as possible are made. This is partly achieved by early feedback of defects found to people like designers and programmers. Another possibility is the use of test cases to validate requirements and design: the system to be designed must be able to process these test cases correctly at a later stage. Also, employing tools optimally is necessary for faster, cheaper, and better testing. From an

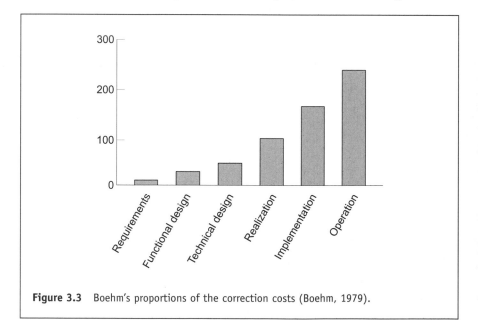

Figure 3.3   Boehm's proportions of the correction costs (Boehm, 1979).

organizational point of view, testing requires special 'testing' skills and should become more professional, with functions such as test managers, method specialists, and engineers. Testware should be managed as a reusable test asset, thereby simplifying retesting. The progress and quality of the total test process should be measured, and the results of these measurements used as input for control of the process or for further test process improvement.

In addition to all of the above, the conceptualization should answer not only the question 'Can we build it?', but also the question 'Can we test it?'. Good *testability* of systems becomes increasingly important. The authors of this book take the position that testability does not refer only to the properties of the IT system itself, as the ISO 9126 definition states:

Attributes of software that bear on the effort needed for validating the modified software

---

but also mainly to the organization and infrastructure of the test process.

CHAPTER 4

A model for test process improvement

If improving the test process takes place in a structured way, generally a number of steps are taken. In going through these steps a frame of reference in the form of a model can give support. Based on the requirements for a model for improving the test process, several existing models can be examined. Because these models provide an insufficient frame of reference, a new model has been developed: the TPI model.

4.1 Improvement steps

What and *why* questions concerning improvement have been described in the previous chapter. The next question we should ask ourselves is *how* to improve. In maintaining the current testing routine, this means just do it, we will achieve a gradual improvement:

- Activities that start off awkwardly will go more smoothly next time.
- Pitfalls will be avoided next time ('once bitten, twice shy').

Improvements can also be implemented in a more structural manner. This approach is much more far-reaching, because the improvements are usually much more extensive and require some form of investment. Although this book is mainly concerned with the latter approach, no negative judgment is passed on the first form; on the contrary: both forms of improvement are complementary and that is why we aim to combine both.

For the structural approach, improving the test process can be compared to the improvement of any other process. Roughly we use the following steps:

1 **Determine target and area of consideration**   We determine what the improvement targets are and what the area of consideration is. Does the testing have to be faster, cheaper, or better? Which test processes are the subject of improvement, how long can the improvement process last, and how much effort can it take?

2 **Determine current situation**   We determine the strong and weak points of the current situation.

3 **Determine required situation**   Based on the analysis of the current situation and the set of improvement targets, we determine the required situation and which improvement actions should be carried out to achieve this situation. A point of interest is that in practice it is usually not possible to implement the required situation at the same moment throughout the organization. Too much at once leads to resistance, insecurity, and chaos, and the result is usually counterproductive: changes are not implemented and there is increased resistance to change within the organization. Also, there are dependencies: some changes are only useful if other improvements have been made. Therefore it is much better to plan the actions in such a way that gradual and step-by-step improvement is possible.

4 **Implement changes**   The suggested improvement actions are performed according to a plan and then a check is made to see if the set of improvement targets has been met. Also, an essential part of this phase is consolidation. We need to see that the organization keeps using the implemented changes, to prevent the changes having a once-only effect.

4.2 Frame of reference

In particular, determining the current and required situation is not easy. What is the current situation and what should the required situation be? Ask a number of people involved in the test process to name strong and weak aspects of the test process and you will get a random number of diverse answers. An even larger number of diverse answers can be expected to the question of what needs to be improved.

For both situations the solution is to use a frame of reference. By comparing the test process to a frame of reference the strong and weak aspects of the test process are more visible. A frame of reference can be a test methodology or a model for (improving) the test process.

A methodology describes a certain design for the test process. An analysis can be done to see to what degree the current test process situation differs from this design. The required situation is usually the complete application of the methodology. When this complete application is not achievable, or cannot be achieved all at once, a partial application is chosen, somewhat arbitrarily.

A model is also focused on the design of a test process, but the aim is not one particular design of test process. The basic principle is that if the test process is designed in a certain way and this design is controlled by the organization, the set improvement targets are met.

In determining the current situation, the degree and manner of the design and its results are examined. Based on this and on the improvement targets, the set of improvement targets to be used is decided.

The advantage of using a model in improving the test process is that it is possible to improve the process gradually and step by step. Trying to implement the required situation with (too) large steps usually leads to failure. Improvement with smaller, controllable steps has a much better chance of success. The reason for this is that change in an organization always encounters problems and resistance. Too many changes at once generate so many problems and so much resistance that it is counter-productive and causes the organization to fall back into old habits.

It is therefore important to implement the change by means of smaller, controllable steps. A model that helps in formulating these steps is very useful. When this model is based on 'best practice' it helps to get everyone on the same track and prevents unnecessary discussions.

4.3 Model requirements

Based on the above-mentioned advantages of a model, a number of requirements can be formulated to which a model must comply. These requirements are described in Table 4.1.

4.4 Available models

Based on these requirements, various existing models can be compared. We look at software process improvement models as well as specific models for test process improvement.

4.4.1 Software process improvement models

A variety of software process improvement models are available. These models address the total development process, that is, from specifying the requirements to building, testing, and so on. Examples are the Capability

Table 4.1 Model requirements.

Requirement	Description
Specific, controlled improvement steps are possible	This is the most important requirement. Specific and controllable steps should be possible, to implement improvements gradually.
Practice-based	The practical use and usefulness of the model are also a requirement of the highest order. This means that it should link to reality and to 'best practice.'
As objective as possible	The model must be sufficiently controllable to be able to determine as objectively as possible what the situation of a test process is and whether the required situation is achieved. Two different persons analyzing the same test process should, within small margins, produce the same results.
Options and priorities	Each test process is different. That is why different choices for improvement have to be made each time. The making of these choices should be supported.
Detailed	To be able to make good use of the model it should contain a high level of detail. It should not be too generic and must be applicable to test processes which are regarded as reasonably 'mature,' but also to test processes which are still 'in their infancy.'
Quick insight of current situation possible	Determining the current situation should be performed relatively quickly and cheaply. Also, an important advantage of this is that it is easier to do interim measurements. These interim measurements are intended to determine the progress of the improvement process.
Independent	In order to be widely applicable, the model should be used regardless of whether an organization tries to improve the total software process or just the test process. The model also has to be independent of any particular test methodology, programming environment or architecture.

Maturity Model (Humphrey, 1989; SEI, 1995), Bootstrap (Kuvaja *et al.*, 1994), SPICE (Emam and Dionin, 1998), and TickIt (Hall, 1995). These models deal with testing, but offer an insufficient frame of reference for step-wise improvement of the test process. As a result of the high level of abstraction, improvement of the test process is often regarded as one single step. That is why they do not, or only partly, meet the requirements for specific and controllable improvement steps.

4.4.2 Test process improvement models

Besides general improvement models, there are some models which are specifically designed for test process improvement. Well-known models are the Testability Maturity Model by David Gelperin (Gelperin, 1996), the Test Improvement Model (TIM) by Ericson, Subotic, and Ursing (Ericson *et al.*, 1996) and the Testing Maturity Model (TMM) by the Illinois Institute of Technology (Burnstein *et al.*, 1996).

Although these models can be used as a frame of reference, the authors of this book aim at a model containing more improvement steps, practical details, and instructions. This is the most important reason for developing a model which is based on practical knowledge and skills and which does meet these requirements: the Test Process Improvement (TPI) model.

CHAPTER 5

The TPI model

The first section of this chapter contains a general description of the model. Then we focus on a number of specific features. Sections 5.3 to 5.7 describe the different parts of the model. The chapter concludes with feedback to the requirements as defined in Section 4.3.

5.1 General description of the TPI model

As already explained in the previous chapter, the TPI model is used to analyze the current situation of a test process and to show its strong and weak aspects. For this it is necessary that the model looks at the test process from different points of view, for example the use of test tools, test specification techniques, and reporting. These are called **key areas**. Examination of each key area leads to classification of the test process into certain **levels** of maturity. The ascending levels improve in terms of time (faster), money (cheaper), and/or quality (better). For example, Table 5.1 lists the levels defined for the key area Reporting, ascending from A to D.

Table 5.1 Levels defined for key area Reporting.

Level	Description
A	Defects found are reported.
B	Progress is reported (tests, products, activities, defects found) and defects are prioritized.
C	The risks for the system and organization are detected and recommendations are made, substantiated with metrics.
D	Recommendations have a Software Process Improvement character.

Because all key areas and levels are not equally important for the performance of the complete test process and because dependencies exist between the different key areas and levels, all key areas and levels are mutually linked in a **Test Maturity Matrix**.

To make sure that the classification into levels is done objectively, one or more **checkpoints** are assigned to each level. A checkpoint is a requirement. If a test process passes all the checkpoints of a certain level, then the process is classified at that level.

In addition to mapping the current situation of the test process, the key areas and levels can also be used to define the required situation and intermediate steps on the way to this situation. As an extra aid **improvement suggestions** have been added to the model giving instructions and suggestions for reaching a certain level.

The model is visualized as shown in Figure 5.1.

We can make an analogy with an exercise program for improving a person's physical condition or performance. The key areas in this case are the different parts of the body: legs, arms, belly, and so on. The levels indicate an ascending degree of speed or strength of the body parts. These levels can be measured using checkpoints, such as being able to lift a certain weight or doing a certain number of exercises in a certain amount of time. An overall improvement in physical performance often depends on the combined performance of more than one body part. Weight-lifting, for example, involves teamwork by body parts such as arms, legs, and belly. The Test Maturity Matrix is a sort of 'results chart' which helps to show the connection between the performance of the different body parts. This prevents one-sided improvement and an individual exercise program can be drawn up, based on the current performance level. Improvement suggestions for reaching a higher performance level are, for example, do specific exercises, eat healthier food, or take steroids.

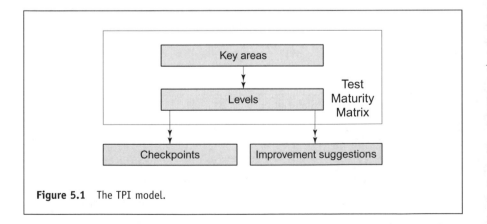

Figure 5.1 The TPI model.

In the next section we deal with key areas, levels, and the Test Maturity Matrix. Chapter 7 describes the levels and the related checkpoints and improvement suggestions in detail.

5.2 Positioning the model

The TPI model has emerged from experience and gives a frame of reference for:

- determining the strong and weak points of the current test process of an organization, and

- formulating specific and realistic improvement actions for this test process.

In the following sections we illustrate a number of factors which have played a role in the realization of the model.

5.2.1 TMap

As a basis for the model the methodology for structured testing, TMap, is used, supplemented with several aspects from the models mentioned in Section 4.4.

The methodology has four cornerstones. These cornerstones are a *life cycle* (*L*) of test activities related to the development cycle, good *organization* (*O*), the right *infrastructure* and *tools* (*I*), and usable *techniques* (*T*) for performing the activities, as shown in Figure 5.2.

The cornerstones are universal, and within each test process some degree of attention must be given to each cornerstone. For a balanced test process, the substantiation of the cornerstones should be in balance. Appendix B contains a short description of TMap.

We emphasize that the implementation of TMap is *not* an end goal of the TPI model, but the details of the methodology are used to provide a model

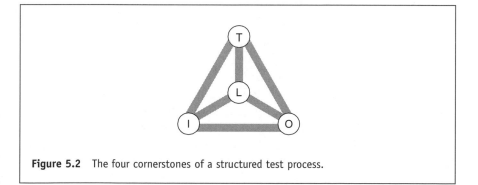

Figure 5.2 The four cornerstones of a structured test process.

which is as complete as possible. Because of this, the model can be applied in organizations that use their own methodology. This methodology will give attention to roughly the same cornerstones and aspects.

5.2.2 Evaluation, high-level and low-level tests

In an 'immature' test process the stimulus for improvement usually comes from the users or system managers of the IT system. They find out (too late) that the IT system that has been accepted is of insufficient quality. The conclusion will be that the test process, especially the later (high-level) tests, for instance the system or acceptance test, has not succeeded in detecting enough of the defects that were present. As a solution, better control of these last test levels is chosen, so that they provide more certainty about and insight into the quality of the system.

Not until this control has been achieved does the efficiency of the test process become more important. The understanding dawns that there is an unnecessary overlap in tests performed at the different test levels and that it saves money and time to take action at an earlier stage of the development process. The most important argument for this is that detecting (and correcting) defects as soon as possible is much cheaper. Both low-level tests and evaluation take place at an earlier stage in the system development phase than high-level tests and therefore are capable of detecting defects closer to their source.

The maturity levels of the key areas connect to the fact that in practice an organization usually starts by focusing on the high-level tests. Initially the levels of the model are concentrated more on these test levels, whereas for a more mature test process the model levels are aimed more at the low-level tests, evaluations, and especially the tuning and integration between all the different sorts of test and evaluation levels.

5.2.3 Administrative automation

The TPI model is mainly designed from knowledge and experience gained within the field of administrative automation. Although testing within this form of automation has much in common with other sorts of automation, such as embedded software or process automation, there are differences. Aspects are more important or less important in those situations, priorities differ, and so on. An example aspect is integration between hardware and software: this is probably less important in administrative automation than in the field of embedded software. It is the responsibility of the person using the TPI model to recognize the similarities and differences and to interpret these correctly.

5.3 Key areas

By looking at the different aspects of each cornerstone under a structured test process, a total of 20 key areas (Figure 5.3) are distinguished for the TPI model. These key areas cover the total test process.

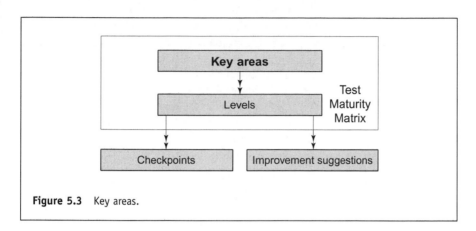

Figure 5.3   Key areas.

The area of consideration of test process improvement usually implies the high-level tests (see also Section 5.2.2). Most key areas are adjusted to this. To give enough attention to the low-level tests and evaluation activities in improving more 'mature' test processes, separate key areas are included for these.

The key areas are described briefly in Table 5.2. The first column shows the cornerstone under which the key area is classified:

L = Life cycle
T = Techniques
I = Infrastructure and tools
O = Organization

Table 5.2 Key areas.

Corner-stone	Key area	Description
L	Test strategy	The test strategy has to be focused on detecting the most important defects as early and as cheaply as possible. The test strategy defines which requirements and (quality) risks are covered by what tests. The better each test level defines its own strategy and the more the different test level strategies are adjusted to each other, the higher the quality of the overall test strategy.

Table 5.2 Key areas (*cont.*).

Corner-stone	Key area	Description
L	Life-cycle model	Within the test process a number of phases can be defined, such as planning, preparation, specification, execution, and completion. In each phase several activities are performed. For each activity the following aspects should be defined: purpose, input, process, output, dependencies, applicable techniques and tools, required facilities, documentation, etc. The importance of using a life-cycle model is improved predictability and controllability of the test process, because the different activities can be planned and monitored in mutual cohesion.
L	Moment of involvement	Although the actual execution of the test normally begins after the realization of the software, the test process must and can start much earlier. An earlier involvement of testing in the system development path helps to find defects as soon and as easily as possible and even to prevent errors. A better adjustment between the different tests can be done and the period of time that testing is on the critical path of the project can be kept as short as possible.
T	Estimating and planning	Test planning and estimating indicate which activities have to be carried out when, and the necessary resources (people). Good estimating and planning are very important, because they are the basis of, for example, allocating resources for a certain time frame.
T	Test specification techniques	The definition of a test specification technique is 'a standardized way of deriving test cases from source information.' Applying these techniques gives insight into the quality and depth of the tests and increases the reusability of the test.
T	Static test techniques	Not everything can and should be tested dynamically, that is, by running programs. Inspection of products without running programs, or the evaluation of measures that must lead to a certain quality level, is called a static test. Checklists are very useful for this.

Table 5.2 Key areas (*cont.*).   **37**

Corner-stone	Key area	Description
T	Metrics	Metrics are quantified observations of the characteristics of a product or process. For the test process, metrics of the progress of the process and the quality of the tested system are very important. They are used to control the test process, to substantiate the test advice, and also to make it possible to compare systems or processes. Why has one system far fewer failures in operation than another system, or why is one test process faster and more thorough than another? Specifically for improving the test process, metrics are important in evaluating the consequences of certain improvement actions, by comparing data before and after performing the action.
I	Test tools	Test tools are automated aids for the test process. Automation within the test process can take place in many ways and has in general one or more of the following aims: • fewer hours needed; • shorter lead time; • more test depth; • increased test flexibility; • more and/or faster insight into test process status; • better motivation of the testers.
I	Test environment	The test execution takes place in a so-called test environment. This environment mainly comprises the following components: • hardware; • software; • means of communication; • facilities for building and using databases and files; • procedures. The environment should be composed and set up in such a way that by means of the test results it can be optimally determined to what extent the test object meets the requirements. The environment has a large influence on the quality, lead time, and cost of the test process. Important aspects of the environment are responsibilities, system management, on-time and sufficient availability, representativeness, and flexibility.

Table 5.2 Key areas (*cont.*).

Corner-stone	Key area	Description
I	Office environment	The test staff need rooms, desks, chairs, PCs, word-processing facilities, printers, telephones, and so on. A good and timely organization of the office environment has a positive influence on the motivation of the test staff, on communication inside and outside of the team, and on the efficiency of the work.
O	Commitment and motivation	The commitment and motivation of the persons involved in testing are important prerequisites for a smoothly running test process. The persons involved are not only the testers, but also, for example, the project management and line management personnel. The latter are mainly important in the sense of creating good conditions. The test process thus receives enough time, money, and resources (quantitatively and qualitatively) to perform a good test, in which cooperation and good communication with the rest of the project result in a total process with optimum efficiency.
O	Test functions and training	In a test process the correct composition of a test team is very important. A mix of different disciplines, functions, knowledge, and skills is required. Besides specific test expertise, knowledge of the subject matter, knowledge of the organization, and general IT knowledge are required. Social skills are also important. For acquiring this mix, training etc. is required.
O	Scope of methodology	For each test process in the organization a certain methodology or working method is used, comprising activities, procedures, regulations, techniques, and so on. When these methodologies are different each time or when the methodology is so generic that many parts have to be drawn up again each time, it has a negative effect on the test process efficiency. The aim is that the organization uses a methodology which is sufficiently generic to be applicable in every situation, but which contains enough detail so that it is not necessary to rethink the same items again each time.

Table 5.2 Key areas (*cont.*).

Corner-stone	Key area	Description
0	Communication	In a test process, communication with the people involved must take place in several ways, within the test team as well as with parties such as the developer, the user, the customer, and so on. These communication forms are important for a smoothly running test process, not only to create good conditions and to optimize the test strategy, but also to communicate progress and quality.
0	Reporting	Testing is not so much 'defect detection' as about giving insight into the quality level of the product. Reporting should be aimed at giving well-founded advice to the customer concerning the product and even the system development process.
0	Defect management	Although managing defects is in fact a project matter and not specifically a matter for the testers, the testers are mainly involved in it. Good management should be able to track the life cycle of a defect and also to support the analysis of quality trends in the detected defects. Such analysis is used, for example, to give well-founded quality advice.
0	Testware management	The products of testing should be maintainable and reusable and so they must be managed. Besides the products of testing themselves, such as test plans, specifications, databases, and files, it is important that the products of previous processes such as functional design and realization are managed well, because the test process can be disrupted if the wrong program versions, etc. are delivered. If testers make demands upon the version management of these products, a positive influence is exerted and the testability of the product is increased.
0	Test process management	For managing each process and activity, the four steps from the Deming circle are essential: plan, do, check, act. Process management is of vital importance for the realization of an optimal test in an often turbulent test process.

The TPI model

Table 5.2 Key areas (*cont.*).

Corner-stone	Key area	Description
(all)	Evaluation	Evaluation means inspecting intermediate products such as the requirements and the functional design. The importance of evaluation is that defects are found at a much earlier stage in the development process than with testing. This makes the rework costs much lower. Also, evaluation can be set up more easily because there is no need to run programs or to set up an environment, etc.
(all)	Low-level testing	The low-level tests are almost exclusively carried out by the developers. Well-known low-level tests are the unit test and the integration test. Just like evaluation, the tests find defects at an earlier stage of the system development path than the high-level tests. Low-level testing is efficient, because it requires little communication and because often the finder is both the error producer and the person who corrects the defect.

5.4 Levels

5.4.1 Description of the levels

In the TPI model, the key areas have a number of levels of maturity (Figure 5.4), A, B, C and so on, where level C is higher than level B and level B is higher than level A. The number of levels is not the same for each key area, but for the sake of applicability there are about three levels per key area.

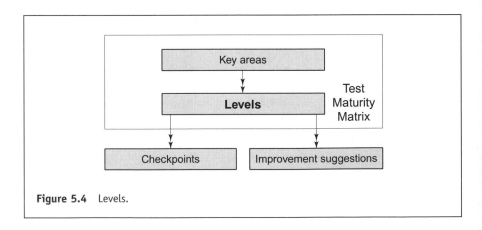

Figure 5.4 Levels.

Each higher level is better than its preceding one in terms of time, money, and/or quality. By using levels we can determine the current situation of a test process and provide better targets for step-by-step improvement.

To be classified for a level, the appropriate checkpoints must be met. The requirements (= checkpoints) of a level also contain the requirements related to the lower levels. A test process classifying at level B for a certain key area meets the requirements of level A as well as level B. When a test process does not meet the requirements of level A, the process is at the starting level. There are no requirements for this lowest level.

In Table 5.3, the levels for the different key areas are displayed. Chapter 7 explains each level, together with the related checkpoints and improvement suggestions.

Below are two examples of what certain levels mean. The precise details of every level can be found in Chapter 7.

EXAMPLE 5.1

For an acceptance test a test strategy is defined, in which a conscious choice is made concerning what parts and aspects of the system are to be tested (and what not), and how thorough these tests are to be (that is, which techniques are to be used). However, there is no coordination with other tests such as the unit, integration, or system tests. This means that the classification of the acceptance test process for the key area Test strategy is on level A.

EXAMPLE 5.2

The test process reports weekly and contains an overview of the defects found and the hours spent. Because the defects have no indication of priority and test progress is not mentioned in the reports, the process is classified for the key area Reporting on level A and not (yet) on level B.

5.4.2 Features

The following features of the higher levels in the TPI model can be mentioned:

- **Growth from project to organization**   The lower levels of the model are focused on a well-set-up test process within a project. Because the nature of projects is a temporary one, on the higher level the model focuses more on the support an organization should structurally give to the organizing of test processes. This prevents the (test process) wheel being reinvented for each project.
  Key areas: Metrics, Scope of methodology, Communication, Test process management.

Table 5.3 Levels.

Key area	Level A	Level B	Level C	Level D
Test strategy	Strategy for single high-level test	Combined strategy for high-level tests	Combined strategy for high-level tests plus low-level tests or evaluation	Combined strategy for all test and evaluation levels
Life-cycle model	Planning, Specification, Execution	Planning, Preparation, Specification, Execution, and Completion		
Moment of involvement	Completion of test basis	Start of test basis	Start of requirements definition	Project initiation
Estimating and planning	Substantiated estimating and planning	Statistically substantiated estimating and planning		
Test specification techniques	Informal techniques	Formal techniques		
Static test techniques	Inspection of test basis	Checklists		
Metrics	Project metrics (product)	Project metrics (process)	System metrics	Organization metrics (> 1 system)
Test tools	Planning and control tools	Execution and analysis tools	Extensive automation of the test process	
Test environment	Managed and controlled test environment	Testing in the most suitable environment	'Environment-on-call'	
Office environment	Adequate and timely office environment			

Commitment and motivation	Assignment of budget and time	Testing integrated in project organization	Test-engineering	
Test functions and training	Test manager and testers	(Formal) Methodical, Technical and Functional Support, Management	Formal internal Quality Assurance	
Scope of methodology	Project specific	Organization generic	Organization optimizing, R&D activities	
Communication	Internal communication	Project communication (defects, change control)	Communication within organization about the quality of the test processes	
Reporting	Defects	Progress (status of tests and products), activities (costs and time, milestones), defects with priorities	Risks and recommendations, substantiated with metrics	Recommendations have a Software Process Improvement character
Defect management	Internal defect management	Extensive defect management with flexible reporting facilities	Project defect management	
Testware management	Internal testware management	External management of test basis and test object	Reusable testware	Traceability system requirements to test cases
Test process management	Planning and execution	Planning, execution, monitoring, and adjusting	Monitoring and adjusting within organization	
Evaluation	Evaluation techniques	Evaluation strategy		
Low-level testing	Low-level test life-cycle (planning, specification and execution)	White-box techniques	Low-level test strategy	

- **Earlier start** Starting testing earlier in the system development means not only that defects can be found earlier, but also that improved cooperation between the different tests and evaluations, and between testing and design/realization, is possible.
  Key areas: Test Strategy, Moment of involvement, Evaluation, Low-level testing.

- **Closer involvement in previous stages** Involving testing in earlier phases such as design and realization has the advantage of better communication and also helps to improve the system's testability. This results in a more efficient test process and timely detection and even prevention of defects.
  Key areas: Moment of involvement, Commitment and motivation, Communication, Reporting.

- **Increasing automation of the test process** Automating the test process gives, after initial investments in time and money, advantages such as shorter lead time, lower costs, and higher quality. However, automation should be seen as a means and not as a goal in itself.
  Key area: Test tools.

- **Professional testing** Testing should receive the attention it deserves. It is expected that the test process is being improved, that the testers give expert advice, and so on. This implies that the people who do this have to be sufficiently capable. Test training, function descriptions, and management support can help to achieve more capable people.
  Key areas: Test functions and training, Commitment and motivation.

5.5 Test Maturity Matrix

See Figure 5.5.

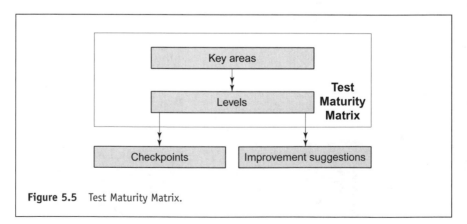

Figure 5.5 Test Maturity Matrix.

5.5.1 Description

In analyzing a test process the level of each key area is determined. Based on these levels, improvements can be suggested in the form of desired higher levels. The temptation can be, for example, to decide to bring all key areas to level B or to say something such as: 'The test process is on level A.' This is definitely not intended, for there are several dependencies and priorities between the levels and the key areas.

> **EXAMPLE 5.3**
>
> Level A of key area Metrics states that metrics are kept per project. This means, for example, that for each unit of time progress, data as well as defect data have to be recorded. Monitoring this data means that the test process for key areas 'Reporting' and 'Defect management' is at least at level B and level A respectively. This implies that 'Metrics,' level A, is dependent on 'Reporting,' level B, and 'Defect management,' level A.

There are such dependencies between many levels and key areas. Section 7.21 contains an overview of all dependencies.

In addition, different priorities can be distinguished. In a very 'immature' test process it is much more important to pay attention to a good test strategy, use of a life-cycle model, and the use of test specification techniques than to collecting metrics, using test tools, or describing the complete test methodology of the project.

Based on the dependencies and priorities, all levels and key areas are mutually related in a Test Maturity Matrix. In the matrix the key areas are indicated vertically and the test maturity scales horizontally. The levels are entered in the boxes. This leads to a matrix with 13 scales of test maturity (Table 5.4).

5.5.2 Matrix

The open boxes between the levels have no meaning as such, but indicate that reaching a higher maturity for the given key area is related to the maturity of other key areas. There is no gradation applied in the model: if a test process is nearly (but not quite) at level B for a certain key area, the process is assigned to level A of that area.

If the test process does not meet level A for a certain key area, the process is set to the zero scale for this key area.

5.5.3 Matrix structure

The scales of test maturity can generally be divided into three categories:

Table 5.4 Test Maturity Matrix.

Key area	0	1	2	3	4	5	6	7	8	9	10	11	12	13
		Controlled					Efficient					Optimizing		
Test strategy	A						B				C		D	
Life-cycle model	A			B										
Moment of involvement		A					B				C		D	
Estimating and planning			A								B			
Test specification techniques	A		B											
Static test techniques					A		B							
Metrics						A			B			C		D
Test tools					A			B			C			
Test environment			A					B						C
Office environment			A											
Commitment and motivation	A				B							C		
Test functions and training			A				B				C			
Scope of methodology				A							B			C
Communication		A		B								C		
Reporting	A			B		C						D		
Defect management	A				B		C							
Testware management		A			B					C				D
Test process management	A		B									C		
Evaluation							A			B				
Low-level testing					A		B		C					

- **Controlled** Scales 1 to 5 are primarily aimed at the control of the test process. The purpose of the levels is to provide a controlled test process, which provides a sufficient amount of insight into the quality of the tested object.

  In real life this means that the test process is carried out in phases according to a strategy defined in advance. Test specification techniques are used for testing, and defects are recorded and reported. The testware and test environment are well controlled and the test staff are adequately trained.

- **Efficient** The levels in scales 6 to 10 focus more on the efficiency of the test process. This efficiency is achieved, for example, by automating the test process, by better integration between the mutual test processes and with the other parties within system development, and by consolidating the working method of the test process in the organization.

- **Optimizing** A test process that is efficient today may not be so tomorrow. Changing circumstances, such as the introduction of new architectures and development techniques, require an adjustment of the test process each time. The levels in the last three scales are characterized by increasing optimization of the test process and are aimed at ensuring that continuous improvement of the generic test process will be part of the regular working method of the organization.

5.5.4 Explanation: tools and metrics

The placing of a number of levels in the matrix is further explained below:

- Perhaps somewhat surprisingly, the use of tools that support test execution, such as Capture & Playback tools, is relatively highly ranked (scale 7). It often happens that the first thought of a customer who wants to improve the test process is to use tools. This view often leads to disappointment because there are many pitfalls, especially in using tools for test execution. In a well-organized process, tools can surely provide an important additional value, but they work counterproductively in an insufficiently organized test process. Various quotes from the literature express this:

  'Automating chaos leads to faster chaos'
  (Graham *et al.*, 1996)

  'Structure then tool'
  (Pol *et al.*, 1995)

  Pitfalls can be, for example, automated testware that is insufficiently maintainable, too much automation, or the tool's incompatibility with the system infrastructure. Also, the investment is typically returned only after a longer period of time, for instance after a couple of tests and retests. This implies that automated testware must have good reusability.

- Although collecting metrics has a high priority in change processes, the first level of metrics in the matrix does not come until scale 5. The reason is that the test process for this (scales 1 to 4) probably cannot deliver metrics yet, and if it can, it certainly cannot use them.

5.5.5 Using the matrix

A Test Maturity Matrix is completed after the analysis of a test process. This gives all concerned a clear view of the levels that the different key areas of the test process are on. By using the matrix it is possible to make a better judgment about improvement actions. Here, the intention is to work from left to right, so that the first objective is to improve the key areas with low test maturity. As a result of the mutual dependencies between the key areas, experience has taught that real peaks (a key area with high test maturity, while the other key areas have low or average maturity) are not very efficient. What is the use of maintaining a very comprehensive defect administration, when this is not used for analysis and reporting? Without acting contrary to the model's principles, it is permissible to deviate from it, but only if there is a good reason.

In the following example three situations are shown; the first is at the start of the improvement process, the second is to be achieved after the first improvement period, and the third is to be achieved after the second improvement period. The improvements follow the 'left-to-right' guideline of the matrix. To keep the example as simple as possible, only a selection of key areas is discussed.

The first situation concerns the acceptance test process and is as follows (Table 5.5):

- The test process does not make a conscious, risk-based choice of what to test and how thoroughly to test it (Test strategy, level < A); instead everything is tested with two home-grown and informal techniques (Test specification techniques, level A).

- It uses a life-cycle model for its activities (level A).

- The process starts around the time that the test basis is completed (Moment of involvement, level A).

- Several kinds of test tools are used (level A).

- Defects found are reported (Reporting, level A).

Table 5.5 Test Maturity Matrix, Situation 1.

Key area	Scale													
	0	1	2	3	4	5	6	7	8	9	10	11	12	13
Test strategy		A					B				C		D	
Life-cycle model		A			B									
Moment of involvement			A				B				C		D	
Test specification techniques		A		B										
Metrics						A			B			C		D
Test tools					A			B			C			
Reporting		A			B		C					D		
Testware management			A			B				C				D
Low-level testing					A		B		C					
etc.														

- The testware produced is not managed well and is insufficiently reusable (Testware management, level < A).

The result is that although a considerable amount of time and resources are given to testing, testing does not offer much insight into the quality of the test object. The test process also requires a lot of rework for each retest to be done, frequently resulting in project delays.

To improve this situation, it is decided to implement the following (Table 5.6):

- The test process is to make a conscious, risk-based choice of what to test and how thoroughly to test it (Test strategy, level A), choosing from a richer set of techniques than those available (Test specification techniques, level B).

- The life-cycle model is extended with activities for inspection of the test basis, giving earlier insight into the quality and testability of the test basis, and for conserving testware and evaluating the process (level B).

- Defects are assigned priorities and reported periodically, together with progress information (Reporting, level B).

- The testware produced is to be managed well by following procedures and making a particular person responsible (Testware management, level A).

This should result in better insight into the quality of the test object and less rework in case of retests.

Table 5.6 Test Maturity Matrix, Situation 2.

Key area	Scale													
	0	1	2	3	4	5	6	7	8	9	10	11	12	13
Test strategy		A					B				C		D	
Life-cycle model		A			B									
Moment of involvement			A				B				C		D	
Test specification techniques		A		B										
Metrics						A			B			C		D
Test tools					A			B			C			
Reporting		A			B	C						D		
Testware management			A			B				C				D
Low-level testing					A		B		C					
etc.														

In the second improvement period, it is decided to broaden the scope of the improvement by involving all test levels, that is, unit, integration, and system tests as well. The following improvements are to be implemented (Table 5.7):

- The acceptance test is to coordinate its strategy with the other high-level test, the system test, thereby preventing gaps or unnecessary overlap in the test coverage (Test strategy, level B). This also places certain demands on the system test, but that is outside the scope of this example.

- Earlier involvement is necessary to be able to coordinate the test strategies effectively (Moment of involvement, level B).

- Metrics are collected and used in reporting (level A).

- Reports contain advice about the quality of the test object. This advice is backed up with statistics (Reporting, level C).

- The test basis and test object are to be managed well by following procedures and making a particular person responsible. As this management is a project responsibility, it is to be done external to the test process (Testware management, level B).

- Low-level tests have to use a life-cycle model and white-box techniques to make their process more manageable and give more quality (Low-level testing, level B).

These improvements will give earlier and more insight into quality, allowing for timely correction measures and less chance of delays caused by insufficient product quality.

Table 5.7 Test Maturity Matrix, Situation 3.

Key area	Scale													
	0	1	2	3	4	5	6	7	8	9	10	11	12	13
Test strategy		A					B				C		D	
Life-cycle model		A			B									
Moment of involvement			A				B				C		D	
Test specification techniques		A		B										
Metrics						A			B			C		D
Test tools					A			B			C			
Reporting		A			B	C						D		
Testware management			A			B				C				D
Low-level testing					A		B	C						
etc.														

5.6 Checkpoints

To determine objectively the level of a key area that a test process is on, the model provides a measuring instrument called checkpoints (Figure 5.6). Each level has a number of checkpoints. A test process must meet these points in order to be classified on that level. These checkpoints are cumulative, which means that for level B the checkpoints for that level must be met, but also the checkpoints for the preceding level A.

Examples of checkpoints are shown in Table 5.8. Chapter 7 gives a complete description of the checkpoints.

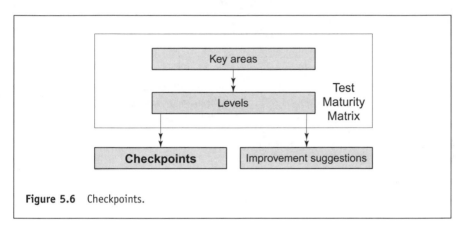

Figure 5.6 Checkpoints.

Table 5.8 Examples of checkpoints.

Key area Test strategy, level A, Strategy for single high-level test	Key area Test strategy, level B, Combined strategy for high-level tests
A motivated consideration of the product risks takes place, for which knowledge of the system, its use and its operational management is required.	Coordination takes place between the different high-level tests, often the system, acceptance and production acceptance tests, in the field of test strategy (risks, quality characteristics, area of consideration of the test, and planning).
There is a differentiation in test depth, depending on the risks and, if present, the acceptance criteria: not all subsystems are tested equally thoroughly and not every quality characteristic is tested (equally thoroughly).	The result of the coordination is a coordinated strategy, which is put in writing. During the total test process this strategy is controlled.
etc.	etc.

5.7 Improvement suggestions

The checkpoints of a certain level are themselves an aid for process improvement. Another aid is the improvement suggestions per level (Figure 5.7). It is emphasized that these suggestions are meant as hints and tips and not as compulsory steps to achieve that level.

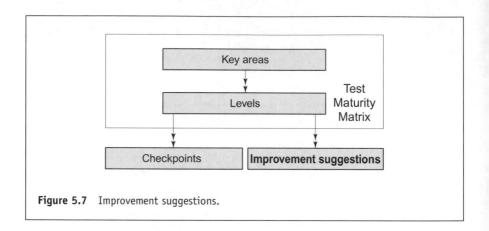

Figure 5.7 Improvement suggestions.

Examples of improvement suggestions are shown in Table 5.9.

Table 5.9 Examples of improvement suggestions.

Key area Test strategy, level A, Test strategy for single high-level test

Involve the various interested parties such as end user, systems manager, and project manager in determining the test strategy.

Create awareness by indicating the risks of the current working method, or indicate how testing can be done more cheaply and/or faster.

etc.

Chapter 7 gives a comprehensive description of the improvement suggestions.

5.8 Properties of the TPI model

Section 4.3 lists a number of requirements that a model must meet. Table 5.10 describes how the TPI model meets these requirements.

Table 5.10 Properties of the TPI model.

Requirement	Description
Specific, controlled improvement steps are possible	Levels have been defined for the different key areas, in which each higher level is seen as an improvement step.
Practice-based	The model matches practice well for the following reasons: • it is based on a practice-proven test methodology; • a high level of detail in combination with the range of choices offered makes the model usable for most real-life situations.
As objective as possible	By means of the checkpoints, it is possible to determine as objectively as possible the level of a key area that a test process is on.
Options and priorities	The different levels and the Test Maturity Matrix offer a lot of support in making the right choices. Also, the improvement suggestions are an important source of ideas and tips to define tailor-made improvement actions.
Detailed	The large number of levels, checkpoints, and improvement suggestions, mainly described in Chapter 7, gives the model a high level of detail.
Fast insight into current situation possible	The checkpoints offer a lot of support for a fast analysis of the current situation. This is an important benefit, both for determining the starting situation of an improvement process and for performing intermediate measurements to determine whether the improvement process is still on schedule.
Independent	An organization can be working on improvement of the total software process (SPI). If SPI models are used for this, there is potential overlap with the TPI model for the test process. The consequences for improving the test process will have to be examined. Most SPI models treat improvement of the test process as one big step. The TPI model can probably assist in breaking down this step into smaller, more controllable steps. The TPI model is independent of any particular test methodology, language, or architecture.

CHAPTER SIX

Application of the TPI model

This chapter deals with the way in which the test process is improved, the change process, and indicates how the TPI model is applied. Then a number of aspects of a change process are discussed, such as the organization, the required knowledge and skills, the expected resistance to changes, and determining the costs and profits of an improved test process. The chapter concludes with an overview of a number of success and failure factors.

6.1 Change process

Each change process consists in general of the same working method: on the basis of targets changes are made to arrive at the required situation from the current situation. Improving the test process does not differ substantially from any other change process. In this section the different activities of a change process are indicated, with special attention to the places where the TPI model can be used.

Figure 6.1 shows the activities of a change process.

The different activities are described in the following sections. Although the diagram gives the impression that they are separate and consecutive activities, there is a certain overlap. Certain activities, such as obtaining awareness, can even be regarded as a continuous activity. A more careful formulation is that the centers of the activities follow each other.

6.1.1 Obtain awareness

The reason for improving the test process generally arises from experiencing a number of problems with testing. The desire is to solve these problems. Improvement of the test process is regarded as the solution.

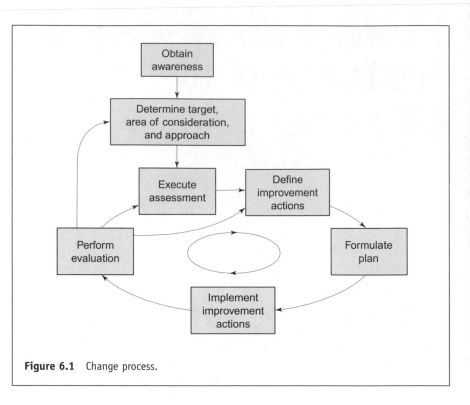

Figure 6.1 Change process.

Important outcomes of this first step (Figure 6.2) are that all parties involved become aware of:

1 the purpose of, and the need for, improvement of the test process, and

2 the fact that a change process using the TPI model is the way to do it.

This awareness implies that the parties mutually agree on the outlines of, and give their commitment to, the change process.

Which parties are initially involved depends entirely on the problems experienced and the selected area of consideration of the change process; for example, senior management, line managers, project managers, test managers, and testers. When at a later stage in the change process the number of parties involved is expanded, the additional parties must also go through this awareness phase.

It is of great importance that the necessity for improvement of the test process is recognized together with the fact that many (large) benefits can be gained from it. If the need for improvement is not recognized, the suggested changes will never be consolidated within the organization and it will tend to fall back into the old working method over and over again.

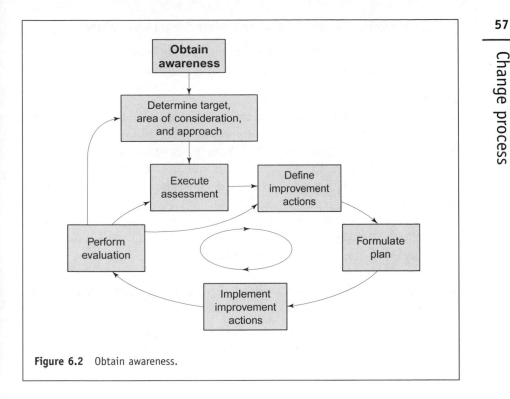

Figure 6.2 Obtain awareness.

The awareness phase should not be regarded as a detached step in the change process, but rather as an essential precondition. If this commitment is insufficient, it is best not to start the change process. The chances of failure are relatively large and when a change process has failed once, the resistance of the organization to the next attempt will be greater.

It is important in this activity that people see that senior management supports the change process. For that reason the process of awareness has to involve senior management at an early stage. Long-term targets and cost/profit issues are discussed with higher management. Problems on the work-floor and short-term improvements are discussed with the testers. When one of these parties is left out, there is a large risk that the test process improvement will fail, especially when a clash between the priorities of the regular work and the change process occurs. Presentations or brainstorming sessions, for example, can be used to obtain the required awareness.

Commitment should not only be acquired at the beginning of the change process, but should be retained throughout all phases of the process. This requires a continuous effort in the form of, for example, information transfer and discussion meetings.

6.1.2 Determine target, area of consideration, and approach

In this activity (Figure 6.3) the target, the area of consideration, and the approach of the change process are defined at a global level.

Target
The ultimate target of TPI is optimizing the required time, money, and quality of testing in relation to the total information services for the organization. This is hard to specify. Yet attempts should be made to define the target in a way which is specific, achievable, mutually consistent, and measurable. A rough indication of the milestones and costs for the target is also given.

Possible targets might be that in a few months or years testing must be X% cheaper, Y% faster, or that there will be Z% less failure in production or in the next test. The problem with such targets is that:

- in practice (objective) data about the current situation often is not available;

- it is difficult to determine to what extent improvement of the test process will lead to the desired targets ('Does introducing test specification techniques lead to Z% fewer failures in production?');

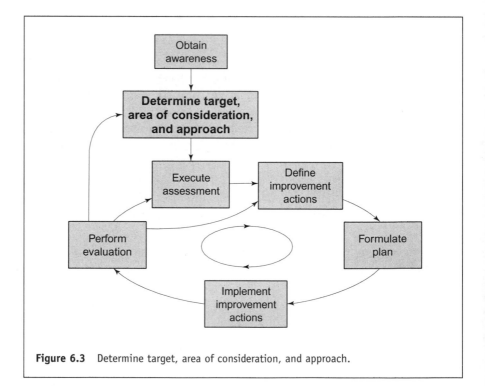

Figure 6.3 Determine target, area of consideration, and approach.

- external factors, such as the quality of the development process, have a profound influence on the quality and efficiency of the test process.

For that reason, most of the time we can give no 'guarantee' that these targets can be met. Instead, we should clearly state the risks and the doubts.

Other targets might be:

- a more transparent and therefore more controllable test process;

- more insight into the quality of the test object by more thorough testing;

- enhanced quality of the advice and timely test advice;

- a shorter training period and better reusability by using a uniform working method;

- making the test process independent of certain persons.

Another point of interest is that the customer of TPI does not always have long-term targets in mind. Often the customer aims at short-term targets such as cost reduction or shortening lead times. In test process improvement it is of the utmost importance that it is clear why the improvement is desired, so that the improvement proposals match the (short-term) targets of the customer.

The reason for improvement might be that testing has to be performed more cheaply in the short term. In that case, measures that require an investment with a longer payback time (for example, measures for improving quality) contribute to the realization of this target to a much lesser degree, and the short-term targets should be emphasized in the proposed measures. It is also recommended to diminish the number of steps in which the test process is improved and to increase the number of times the progress of the improvement process is measured. In such (one-sided) process improvement, the related risks should be clearly indicated (for instance, because no quality-improving measures are taken, the risk remains that not until production has started will it become clear that the quality of the product is insufficient). The advantage of process improvement with short-term targets is that the basis for further improvement gradually increases, especially if it appears that the measures are effective.

EXAMPLE 6.1

In a medium-sized financial institution a crucial IT system is to be replaced. A project-based approach is chosen where the project is responsible for the total replacement of the system. Within the project sub-projects are started, which have the task of replacing a certain part of the system. This will avoid the negative effects of a 'big bang,' a sudden replacement of the old system by the new system, but instead leads to a gradual replacement of the old subsystems by newly built subsystems.

A very chaotic test process preceded the delivery of the first subsystems, which turned out to be of a disappointing quality.

To bring more structure into the test process, the head of the system development department calls in an external test advisor for the project. This advisor does research and gives advice with a number of short- and long-term recommendations. The short-term recommendations, which can be implemented with little time or costs, are accepted quickly. The long-term recommendations (among them the use of certain test techniques) are discussed with the project manager and the head of the system development department.

After providing this advice the advisor gets another assignment: to support a test leader for a test process which is to be started. Short-term recommendations have been taken over from the previous test process, and in addition a number of other improvements have been applied.

The test path runs more smoothly, but the advisor senses that nothing is being done with the long-term recommendations. Because the next subsystems to be delivered are becoming increasingly complex, integration is becoming a more important aspect, and the tester's knowledge about these subsystems is less, the advisor points out again that only applying short-term recommendations is not enough to overcome future problems. The answer the advisor gets is that the investments in time (and to a lesser extent, money) are not achievable for the time being. The project needs all available resources, and training on how to use the test techniques is not possible. Although the advisor argues that the current working method is not sufficient for the subsystems to be tested in the future and that there is a substantial risk of an uncontrolled test process that will exceed time limits, there is not enough commitment for the project.

Later it turns out that the test process is again problematic and very much behind schedule.

The moral

It turned out that the experience drawn from the first sub-projects was not applied thoroughly enough when the next sub-projects showed a (temporary) improvement. Within a project which is under a lot of time pressure (and which project isn't!) it is very hard to implement structural improvements. Often the required investment in time and/or money is not acceptable to the project management. This is partly founded on 'wishful thinking,' because management hopes that the risks at which the measures are aimed do not become reality. Also, the project management is often mainly judged on the time and money spent and to a lesser extent on the quality of the delivered system. This is not a stimulus for investing in measures that improve quality.

The area of consideration of the change process has several possibilities:

- one test level in a project (for example, the system test in project X);

- all test levels in a project;

- all tests of a certain test level in the entire organization (for example, all acceptance tests);

- all test levels in the entire organization.

A limited area of consideration causes limited possibilities for the improvement of the test process. When the area of consideration is one test level, for example the acceptance test, in one project, little influence can be exerted on the other tests within that project. On the other hand, the risk will be substantial that in the next project a start will have to be made from scratch. Improving a test process with such an area of consideration should be aimed at short-term improvements. The lower level of the TPI model especially can offer support here, but it is for the user of the model to decide the correct short-term measures.

Approach

Although in all cases the consecutive steps of the change process have to be taken, the interpretation of each step is largely dependent on the chosen (short- or long-term) targets and on the area of consideration. This has implications for the change process approach. In a change process with limited targets and area of consideration it is possible to implement the change within a short time frame. The costs are low and the number of people involved is small. An implication of this is that far less attention has to be given to acquiring and sustaining commitment than in a change process that aims to improve all test processes in an organization.

To control the change process it is vital that the change takes place in fairly small steps. Using the TPI model gives support in choosing these steps in the form of key areas, levels, and the Test Maturity Matrix. Besides the changes concerning the content of the test process, the change process itself should also be guided. How the change process is organized, who is responsible, how progress monitoring will take place, and so on, are defined.

The results of this step should be recorded in a document, which is continuously expanded or adapted using the results of further steps.

6.1.3 Execute assessment

In the assessment activity (Figure 6.4), research is done to establish the strong and weak points of the current situation. Based on the target defined

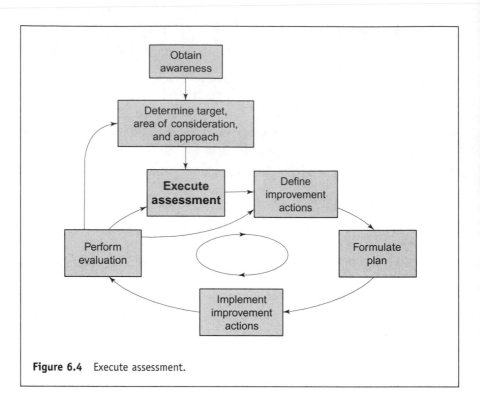

Figure 6.4 Execute assessment.

earlier and the current situation, the change actions are determined in the next activity. The use of the TPI model is an important part of the assessment, because it gives a frame of reference for listing the strong and weak aspects of the test process.

'If you don't know where you are, a map won't help'

(Humphrey, 1989)

If a large number of test processes are part of the area of consideration of the change process, often the observation is that each test process uses its own working method for testing. In that case, the assessment approach can be aimed at starting with an analysis of a representative part of the test processes. The average of these different analyses can be used to produce a picture of the current test maturity of the organization. On the basis of this, global improvement actions can be formulated in the next activity of the change process. Then the current situation can be analyzed for each individual test department, organization, or process and the global improvement actions can be refined to that specific situation.

An assessment consists of a number of steps, which are explained below:

- preparation;
- collecting information;

- analysis;

- reporting.

Preparation

In the first step the person or group of persons who perform the assessment (the assessors) determine who will participate in the assessment, which documentation is to be used, and in which form and when the assessment is to take place.

In the preparation of interviews it is determined who is to be asked about which key areas.

Examples of the documentation to be gathered and studied are test plans and reports, test scripts, defect administration, and procedures, norms, and standards for testing.

Management participation in the assessment is important in order to get commitment. If management is not involved and they are suddenly confronted with the results, the risk exists that the degree of acceptance is too low. Other participants are chosen from the testers, test managers, project leaders, developers, system managers, and end users.

Collecting information

By interviewing the participants, studying the documentation, and optionally by witnessing the process, the necessary information is collected.

If the person who is interviewed gives too positive or too negative an account of the situation, a biased view can be presented. The interviewer should be aware of this. Studying the documentation can help to recognize this bias.

Also, the assessor(s) should be able to guarantee that all information gathered from interviews will be treated confidentially. This is to give those interviewed faith in the manner in which their information is handled, so that they do not feel inhibited in giving their opinions.

Analysis

On the basis of the collected data, the levels per key area of the TPI model are examined by using checkpoints and it is determined which checkpoints were met, not met, or only partially met. This requires a clear argument. A key area has a certain level if:

1 all checkpoints of that level are met, and

2 all checkpoints of preceding levels are met.

In the interviews during the assessment, often problems are found that are not related to the test process, for example a high staff turnover rate, an uncontrolled building process, or a new building approach (for example, Rapid Application Development or object-oriented development) that does

Table 6.1 Example assessment Test Maturity Matrix.

Key area	Scale													
	0	1	2	3	4	5	6	7	8	9	10	11	12	13
Test strategy		A				B					C		D	
Life-cycle model		A		B										
Moment of involvement			A			B					C		D	
Estimating and planning				A							B			
Test specification techniques		A	B											
Static test techniques					A	B								
Metrics						A		B			C			D
Test tools					A		B			C				
Test environment			A				B							C
Office environment			A											
Commitment and motivation		A			B						C			
Test functions and training			A				B		C					
Scope of methodology					A						B			C
Communication			A	B							C			
Reporting		A			B	C					D			
Defect management		A				B	C							
Testware management			A			B				C				D
Test process management		A	B								C			
Evaluation							A			B				
Low-level testing					A		B		C					

not meet expectations. It would be wrong to do nothing with these findings. A solution is to separate them out, and then discuss with the customer what can be done with them.

Reporting

The analysis results are recorded. The Test Maturity Matrix is used here to give a status overview of the test process. This will show the strong and weak aspects of the test process in the form of assigned levels of key areas and their position in the matrix.

An example of a filled-in matrix is given in Table 6.1. The shaded boxes indicate the test process levels for this example.

6.1.4 Define improvement actions

On the basis of the improvement targets and the results of the assessment, the improvement actions are determined (Figure 6.5). The actions are

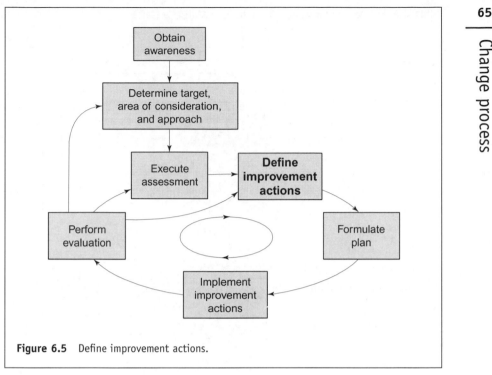

Figure 6.5 Define improvement actions.

determined in such a way that a gradual and step-by-step improvement is possible. The fact is that in practice it is not possible to implement the desired end situation in the entire company at the same time.

The TPI model helps to set up these improvement actions. The levels of the key areas and the Test Maturity Matrix give several possibilities for defining gradual improvement steps. Depending on the targets, the area of consideration, the lead time, and the assessment results, the choice to carry out improvements for one or more key areas can be made. For each selected key area a decision can be made to go to the next level or, in special cases, even to the next-higher level.

Table 6.2 gives an example result of long-term improvement actions. The lightly shaded boxes indicate the current levels, the darker shaded boxes the required levels.

In addition, the TPI model offers a large number of improvement suggestions which help to achieve higher levels.

Other criteria that can be used in determining improvement actions are:

- fast, visible results;
- low costs;
- easiest actions first;

Application of the TPI model

Table 6.2 Example improvement actions Test Maturity Matrix.

Key area	Scale 0	1	2	3	4	5	6	7	8	9	10	11	12	13
Test strategy		A					B				C		D	
Life-cycle model		A		B										
Moment of involvement			A				B				C		D	
Estimating and planning				A							B			
Test specification techniques		A	B											
Static test techniques					A		B							
Metrics						A			B			C		D
Test tools					A			B			C			
Test environment			A					B						C
Office environment			A											
Commitment and motivation		A				B						C		
Test functions and training				A			B			C				
Scope of methodology					A						B			C
Communication			A		B							C		
Reporting		A			B		C					D		
Defect management		A				B		C						
Testware management			A			B				C				D
Test process management		A		B								C		
Evaluation							A			B				
Low-level testing					A		B		C					

- acceptance level in the organization;

- best cost/profit ratio;

- decrease highest risks.

To what extent these criteria play a role in the overall process is totally dependent on factors such as the targets set, the level of acceptance of the change process, and the available knowledge and means.

The improvement actions should be in accordance with and lead to the achievement of the targets set earlier for the improvement of the test process. This is one of the most complex aspects of improvement. How can it be determined that the implementation of a number of actions leads to the achievement of previously defined targets? Achieving certain levels of key areas usually cannot guarantee that these targets are achieved, not least because all sorts of external factors have an influence on achieving those targets. For that reason it is important that the defined targets can be measured in some way or another and that periodically measurements are taken to see whether the improvement actions give the desired result and to what extent the targets are met.

Especially in long-term improvement processes, sometimes multiple improvement cycles are defined, each of which comprises a certain number of improvement actions. The division into improvement cycles is intended to keep the entire change process controllable. It helps to prevent insight into progress being lost because many individual improvement actions must be performed over a long period of time. A cycle goes through the phases of planning, implementation, and evaluation, so that when a cycle ends, the next planned cycle can start or adjustments can be made. The usual duration of a cycle is between a few months and a year.

For each improvement action the budgeted costs, dependencies, and priorities are defined. The improvement cycle to which the action belongs is also indicated.

6.1.5 Formulate plan

A plan is drawn up (Figure 6.6) to implement (a part of) the improvement actions in the short term. The objectives are recorded in this plan and the

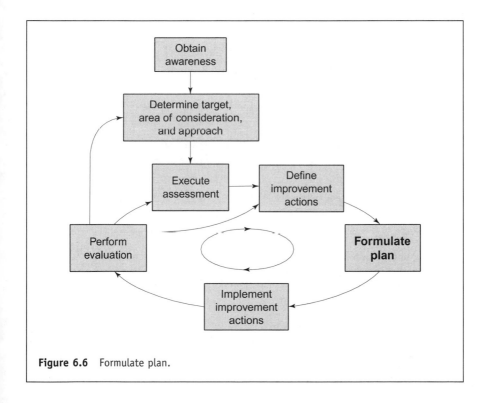

Figure 6.6 Formulate plan.

plan indicates which improvements have to be implemented at what time to realize these aims.

The plan has to answer the following questions:

- Who is the customer?

- Who took on the assignment and/or is responsible for the implementation?

- What is (the area of consideration of) the assignment?

- Which improvement actions are to be taken?

- How will these actions be implemented?

- What are the milestones for implementing the improvement actions?

- Who and what is needed and when?

- How much does it cost?

- What results should the action produce (for example, in the form of products)?

- How often and at what (intermediate) times will progress be measured?

- What are the risks and what is done to make them controllable?

The plan deals with the activities with respect to the content of test process improvement as well as activities needed to steer the change process in the right direction.

Possible activities in the first category are (not exhaustive):

- **Select and use pilot projects** to implement the improvement actions on a small scale and in a manageable environment first.

  In choosing pilot projects it must be considered whether the projects are suitable. A project that is under heavy time pressure is a less suitable candidate, because improvement actions that require an initial investment in time and money will perish first when the pressure becomes too high. Do not choose only one project, because a setback in this project can instantly delay the entire change process; equally, do not choose too large a number of projects, because supporting these can be labor-intensive and adjustment will become difficult.

- **Training** Merely training is not enough: 'We'll send them on a three-day course and then they have to do it on their own.' Training provides a good basis, but then knowledge has to be extended by on-the-job training, mentoring, coaching, and periodic evaluation.

- **Adapting procedures and manuals** Here also, it is not enough to put a new version of the manual on the shelf. Books and procedures must actually be used. Therefore, do not take it for granted that the procedures on paper represent the reality.

- **Purchasing and implementing tools** The word 'tools' often suggests a productivity increase of tens of percent or more. These expectations often need to be corrected, because in practice the figures relate to very specific situations and not to the test process as a whole.

  The purchasing of tools should not be regarded as redemption money: 'I spent tons of cash on those tools and now I don't want to be bothered with it anymore.' Process improvement is more than a one-time investment and continuously requires management commitment.

- **Employing test experts** These experts can give the required support in many activities. Prevent situations in which external test experts train and coach external testers, and then, when the project is finished, both parties leave and the organization does not benefit at all. The target should be to implement improvements and to consolidate these within the organization.

Possible activities to keep the change process into the right track are:

- **Presentations** All sections of the organization involved must be informed about the changes. Presentations are a suitable form of communication for this. Should commitment not be obtained, or if are there many uncertainties concerning the road that must be taken, the next form of communication is more suitable.

- **Discussion meetings** It is better to expose possible resistance beforehand in a systematic manner than to deny or trivialize it. In such meetings, those involved can, on the one hand, be convinced of the use of a change and, on the other, be a source of ideas and problems which had not been thought about. A passive variant on the last-mentioned point is the introduction of a suggestion box. With ideas and problem-solving measures, the change process can run more smoothly and commitment to change is increased.

- **Participation in consultative bodies** Periodic participation in consultative bodies keeps the improvement process in the spotlight. Too often we see that initially a test process improvement is introduced with great fanfare, but then silence ensues. When, after a long time, the change team is again in the public eye with their products, interest has faded and nobody is enthusiastic about working with these products.

- **Kick-off meetings** Upon starting an implementation of improvement actions, a kick-off meeting is organized with the group of people directly involved. The activities to be performed in the short term, the target of these activities, and who should do what at which time are spelt out. Now, everyone has a clear view of what should happen, which makes coordination and cooperation a lot easier.

- **Publications** Publications, booklets, posters, or reference cards are often an easy (and cheap) way to reach a far larger audience than can be reached using presentations. Apart from obtaining commitment, this form is very suitable for continuing commitment, for example by writing articles about the progress of the change process from time to time.

6.1.6 Implement improvement actions

The plan is executed (Figure 6.7). Because the consequences of the change process have the most impact in this phase, much effort should be spent on communication. This emphasizes the attention to such activities in the previous phase. Those involved should be very well informed about the what, why, and how of the actions that are to be performed. Also, this group should feel strongly committed to the execution. A means of achieving

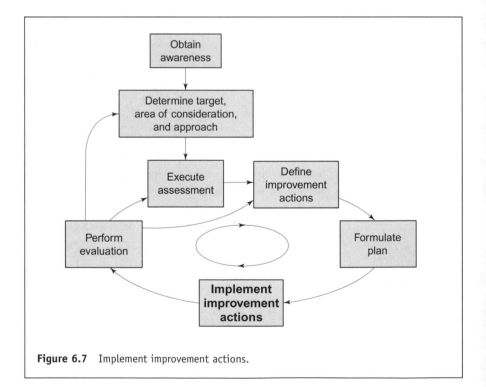

Figure 6.7 Implement improvement actions.

this is the creation of communication channels in which information requests, suggestions, problems, and ideas can be brought to attention. Resistance, which undoubtedly is present, must be brought to the surface and discussed. In addition, clearly visible management commitment is a help.

The executed actions have to be measured to determine to what extent they have been executed. Mechanisms for this are 'self-assessments,' in which the TPI model is applied to quickly determine the status of the test process. Here, those involved inspect their own test process by means of the TPI model. A disadvantage of this working method is that the risk of subjective bias is larger than in the case of the 'normal' assessment.

Based on these results, a statement can be made about the progress of the change process. Also, a vital part of this phase is consolidation. Steps should be taken to prevent the implemented improvement actions having a once-only effect. The organization must continue to use the changed working method. Communication of the results, courses, training, and a quality system can support this.

6.1.7 Perform evaluation

To what extent did the implemented actions give the intended result? In this phase (Figure 6.8) the aim is to see to what extent the actions were

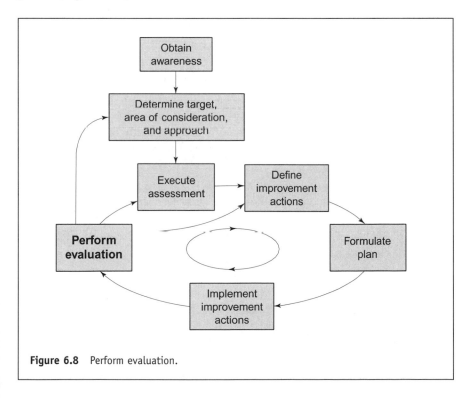

Figure 6.8 Perform evaluation.

implemented successfully as well as to what extent the initial targets were met. Based on these observations, the change process can continue in any number of ways:

- The next improvement cycle is started.

- The improvement actions are adjusted.

- A new assessment is executed, after which the change process is continued from there with the definition of improvement actions, formulation of plans, and so on.

- New targets or areas of consideration are determined, after which the change process continues from there.

- Further improvement of the test process is stopped.

6.2 Quick scan

Besides the application of the above-mentioned complete change process, the TPI model can also be used on a more limited scale within a special form of assessment, the quick scan.

In a quick scan a TPI expert performs a relatively light assessment, which results in a number of recommendations and thus forms the end product. Activities preceding the assessment, such as obtaining awareness and determining target, area of consideration, and approach, are performed minimally. The main use of a quick scan is that the organization is given a quick insight into the quality of its own test process, because this process is compared to a frame of reference (in this case the TPI model). On the basis of this insight the organization could decide to implement the recommendations, but it does not decide in advance, contrary to a regular change process, that there will be changes.

A quick scan is preferred if, for example, the organization is more interested in short-term results than in results that are only advantageous in the longer term (even if these advantages are possibly much larger), or when it is not clear that the improvement of the test process will actually lead to the desired results.

6.3 Organization of the change process

The area of consideration plays a particularly important role in arranging the organization of the change process. When this area is relatively limited, the choice can be made to set up a single change team or project. This team largely handles the planning, preparation, execution, and monitoring of all activities from obtaining awareness to evaluation. Only the actual implementation activities are, as a rule, performed by those involved in the test process.

When the area of consideration concerns a large organization with more departments or test levels, a decision can be made to delegate some of the responsibilities and tasks. A change team continues to exist centrally, but a number of decentralized teams are also formed. The central group handles the obtaining of awareness, target definition, the area of consideration and the approach, the assessment, and the formulation of improvement actions. For both assessment and the formulation of improvement actions, the central change team defines the scope and guidelines. Decentralized groups perform the activities on the basis of these scopes and guidelines in more detail and are responsible for the following activities, 'formulate plan' to 'perform evaluation.' The central group deals with giving support, coordinating and monitoring the sub-activities, keeping commitment going, and evaluating the results achieved on a more general level.

The strong aspect of decentralization is that involvement in the change process is much higher. There can be much more participation in the suggested improvements. The drawback is that too much decentralization hinders integration. Each decentralized team occupies itself with changes which are improvements for its own situation, but which are possibly not for the organization as a whole.

An important aspect of organizing a change process is who will pay the bill. A change process in which each department or project has to bear the cost of the changes itself has very little chance of succeeding. Which project leader feels the need to implement changes using his or her project's budget when only later projects will benefit from them? The same applies, albeit to a somewhat lesser extent, to departments. Some departments will have to bear the costs of changes that are cost-effective for the organization as a whole, but mean extra expenses for themselves. The solution is to address the particular management level where the cost and profit of a test process come together. A change process is usually not cost-effective immediately and always causes a shift in costs as well as profits. It is important to keep this in mind from the very beginning, to minimize the chance that the changes are resisted from a cost point of view.

EXAMPLE 6.2

In a large financial organization the decision is made to improve the test process. The main aim is that testing should be faster and cheaper, without losing quality. The customers are a staff department and an IT department. In the change process the TPI model is used as a frame of reference. All high-level tests are part of the area of consideration of the improvement process. The lead time of the change process is estimated at one and a half to two years.

Initially, an assessment is performed. Several interviews and documentation studies form an image of the current situation of the test processes. Based on this image (in which, for example, the Test Maturity Matrix offers help) several improvements are suggested. In general it is determined that the different test processes should have reached a certain scale of test maturity in one and a half years' time. One of the most important improvements which is suggested is that the different test levels have to be better adjusted to and integrated with one another. In the current situation it appears that there is much unnecessary overlap between the test levels.

After the presentation of these general plans, it is now up to the different parts of the organization to turn these aims into concrete plans for their specific situation. A central change team is in charge of coordinating and monitoring these change processes.

Although several presentations and awareness sessions have been held to generate the needed commitment and although everyone is enthusiastic, it quickly turns out that the whole process is progressing with difficulty. The departments of the organization are not able to realize the concrete plans within the set time and it appears that they are busy implementing the smaller and easier improvements, while the most important recommendations are left out. In the analysis two important problems turn up:

1   It is expected of the different parts of the organization that they improve the test process out of their own budget. So far, certain staff departments have been used as contacts between the change team and the various departments. However, the management layer responsible for budgeting is not involved in the change process. Acquiring budgets causes many problems.

2   Adjusting the different test levels implies that the different parts of the organization must consult each other on how to organize this. The organizational culture causes problems: there is a great deal of mutual distrust and a lack of guidance 'from the top.'

The measure that is taken is that the change process steps back a bit and tries again to get commitment from the appropriate management level. Also, a proposal is made to expand the existing steering committee with (a number of) these managers. Besides the general progress of the change process, the specific problems concerning mutual integration is part of the area of attention of that steering committee.

Lesson

The change organization must be related to the area of consideration of the improvement actions. For actions that require integration of different parts of the organization, the commitment of the managers responsible is vital.

6.4 Required knowledge and skills

The change team must have a mixture of knowledge and skills:

- social skills such as:
  - ability to advise;
  - conflict handling;
  - ability to negotiate;
  - enthusiasm and persuasiveness;
  - honest and open attitude;
  - panic- and criticism-proof (shock-proof);
  - patience;

- profound knowledge about the organization in general;

- profound knowledge about the test process in the organization;

- profound knowledge about and expertise of change processes;

- profound test expertise;

- good knowledge of the TPI model.

This mix will almost never be present in one person. In composing the group it must be ensured that the appropriate knowledge and skills are present in the team. It is most preferable for the change team leader to be part of the organization itself and not an external test advisor, because the aim is not that an external advisor is 'the driving force,' but that this force is in the organization. The reason for this is that otherwise there is a much higher risk that losing the external expert results in the organization falling back into the old situation.

For performing the assessment, on the other hand, the use of external assessors is preferred. These people have a fresh and objective outlook on the state of affairs, because they have experience of other organizations. An internal assessor is much more often regarded as partial. A second reason is that the assessor can be looked upon as the bearer of bad tidings. This happens especially when the assessment results cause much resistance. This can personally harm and stigmatize an internal assessor. In case of an external party this is less important.

A point of interest in the composition of the change team is the availability of the people. Particularly for internal personnel who are assigned part-time to a change process, the dilemma is between their regular everyday tasks and the change activities, sometimes called going-concern and growing-concern. Under time pressure, regular work is usually given priority over improvement process activities, with the result that the change process comes to a dead end.

Below, some personality features of the change team participants are explained in more detail.

6.4.1 Perseverance next to enthusiasm and persuasiveness

It is important that the participants are themselves convinced of the need to change. It is often the case that the desired change does not take shape fast enough. This may lead to the notion that the change is not possible anyway. The great danger in this is that it becomes a self-fulfilling prophecy: the participants interpret the signal as indicating that the organization does not want to implement the changes. Finally this influences their attitude in such a way that they are not capable of convincing others to implement the changes.

What these people can do about this attitude is look for positive signals that indicate that change is desired. The mere fact that a change process is started is an important signal that there is an actual need for change.

6.4.2 Honest and open attitude

Another point of interest is attitude. A cooperative attitude is much more productive than the arrogance of the know-it-all. Take problems and people seriously. In general, those involved in a test process have good knowledge of what they are doing, are doing their best, have tried all sorts of things, and do not appreciate it if someone tells them how they should do their work. A cooperative attitude gives people the feeling that the improvement is a joint action and that their participation is valued appropriately.

6.5 Resistance

The phenomenon of resistance is often underestimated. Where changes take place, there will be some people bluntly against these changes. All kinds of reasons exist for not being enthusiastic about the change process. The change team should be able to handle this; they should actively reduce resistance. This requires insight into the relationship between the phase the change process is in and the behavior of the change team and the amount of resistance engendered. Resistance can be predicted and influenced.

At the start of the change process only a few people are informed. Resistance can only increase if the change plans and their influence are made known. After publication, adequate support and tools must be available to reduce resistance. During execution and support, test personnel produce improvement proposals. These must be taken into account and, if necessary, negotiations carried out. Listening attentively and accepting the proposals reduces resistance considerably. Continuous support convinces

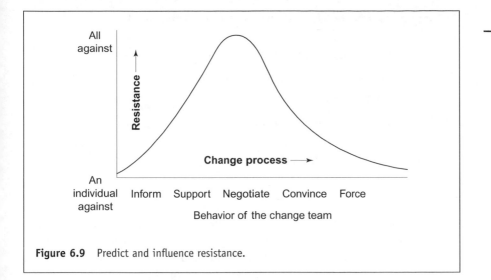

Figure 6.9 Predict and influence resistance.

the testers in this phase of the use of changes. They will convince their indecisive colleagues and even force them to cooperate. By giving information, not too late but certainly not too soon, the resistance curve can be influenced. For example, before people are informed extensively, resistance-reducing facilities such as support and tools must be available. By making forecasts about which type of resistance a certain action will invoke, reducing measures can be taken beforehand each time. Thus resistance can be influenced (see Figure 6.9).

An important message of the above is that all the stages *must* be performed. When the process has reached the implementation phase of improvement measures and still no resistance can be detected, the most plausible reason is that nothing is being implemented! This is the reason for bringing resistance to the surface and debating it, instead of letting it fester beneath the surface.

When a previously started change process has failed, resistance in the organization to future changes is larger than it initially was. Why should the process succeed the second time? This is one of the many reasons not to start a change process without thorough preparation.

6.6 Costs and profits

An important subject of a change process is to what extent the defined targets are met and to what extent the profits of the change process are higher than its costs. Unfortunately this is also one of the most difficult subjects. The reason for this is that both the costs and the profits are hard to determine.

Certain costs of the change process can be determined:

- Costs of the change team and its activities.
- Costs of the presentations, meetings, etc. that those involved must attend for the change process.
- Necessary means such as tools, training, etc.

Costs that are more difficult to determine are:

- Training time and training on the job.
- Extra activities initiated by the change process in the test process ('At first three people began working three weeks before the production date, now suddenly we have to make a plan and prepare test cases, causing three people to start five weeks before the production date').

Determining the profits is the most difficult. Profits are:

- **Higher system quality** But what is higher quality? Fewer failures in production? Better or worse than what? And is it because the tester tests better or because the developer develops better?

- **Higher test quality** How do we know that a better test is performed? The number of reported defects or the number of production failures is not a good criterion, because the developer has a large influence on these factors.

- **Better information about the quality of the system and the risks of taking the system into production** How much is this information worth? Can this be quantified in relation to the costs?

- **Shorter lead time or lower costs of the test process and of the overall project** Shorter or lower than what? Important factors for lead time and costs are the size, importance, and complexity of the system. This determines how many tests must be performed and how thoroughly. Also, the initial quality of the system is usually an unknown factor at the beginning: the higher the quality, the faster and more cheaply the test process can be performed.

- **Reusable testware** This means that the next release costs less test effort than is usually the case for a next release. But each system has a different size, importance, and complexity. Each release has its different adaptations. The amount of changes made in the system influences the testware's reusability level.

- Other benefits that can be mentioned are: better process control, better motivation of the testers, better communication between testers and the rest of the project, higher customer satisfaction, and more confidence in the quality of the tested product. These items are all difficult to quantify.

Although the above-mentioned factors illustrate the difficulties of determining costs and profits, there are solutions to this problem.

In the key area Metrics several metrics are indicated which cover the quality, costs, and lead time of the test process. Examples of metrics are the number of defects per hour, the percentage of code covered by test cases, and the number of defects found in a test in relation to the number of defects present. Combined use of metrics can give a good insight into the profits deriving from the improvement. Such metrics are by far the most objective way to determine the profits of the improved test process.

However, there are a number of disadvantages related to the use of these metrics, which in practice get in the way of large-scale application. The first disadvantage is that, in order to be able to make a comparison, data is required concerning the before-situation as well as the after-situation. Data concerning the before-situation is usually not available, because at that time nobody saw the need to collect it. Also, the working method of the test process has to be adapted for the collection and use of metrics. This implementation of metrics is often regarded as a change process in its own right (whose costs are even more difficult to measure, though).

In addition to metrics, 'common sense' plays an important role in showing the profits and, more generally speaking, the more subjective criteria. By means of, for example, evaluation meetings and interviews the profits of an improved test process can be made visible in a more subjective way. In determining the targets the limitations and uncertainties of the more subjective approach must be indicated clearly, so that everyone knows them and accepts this working method.

6.7 Critical factors

To conclude this chapter a number of factors are indicated which are of great importance for the success of the change process. These factors are divided into success and failure factors.

6.7.1 Success factors

- **Need for change** When a change process is started, an important precondition is that the current situation is recognized as not acceptable. The different layers in the organization should be convinced that the test process must be improved.

- **Clarity of the required situation** The change process should have a clearly defined target, so that it is clear to everyone what must be achieved. These targets can differ for each target group. For senior management the target is, for example, to shorten the time-to-market for new products, for the testers that fewer (boring) retests are needed. The different target groups should have in view the targets that are relevant to them.

- **Sponsor commitment** Probably the most important success (and failure) factor is management commitment to the change process. The impatience of management helps in getting commitment to change an organization, but can have a wrong effect when the expectations created are not realized fast enough. When it is not clear that the management supports the change process, this has to be changed. Steps should be taken to prevent change processes being released into the organization as tentative suggestions.

- **Change team participants** Using the right people to control and guide the change process is of great importance for good progress of the process.

  These people must create an open atmosphere, in which there are no inhibitions about giving ideas or criticism. They are preferably employed full-time in the change process and have no other activities. Otherwise, there is a large chance that when other activities are pressed for time, the first victim is participation in the change process.

  The status of the (internal) people who are employed to implement the change is also a signal to the rest of the organization concerning the importance of the change process. Are 'heavyweights' being used, or people who are insufficiently qualified for the 'regular' work?

  The assessors should have ample (test and change) experience. They should give attention to the specific problems of the test process instead of merely formulating the general model recommendations.

- **Dealing with resistance** Earlier we indicated that all changes will meet resistance. The degree of resistance also depends on, among other things, the culture of an organization – to what extent the organization is used to changing. Make management aware of the fact that this resistance will (and must) always arise and prevent it from causing stagnation of the change process and the disappearance of commitment. To overcome this resistance, it is strongly advised that as many people as possible should be involved in the change process and made stakeholders in it. Lack of understanding about the importance of changes increases the resistance factor.

- **Anticipate future events** Often events that have consequences for the change process occur outside the area of consideration of the change process. Under pressure it becomes clear how mature the test process in fact is. Are all changes immediately thrown overboard when a fire is being put out, or do we sail on a bit more slowly in case of a head wind? Considering a number of scenarios beforehand (how are we going to react if that happens?) can help to prevent everything being thrown overboard.

6.7.2 Failure factors

- **Exclusive top-down or bottom-up improvement** Improvement is said to be top-down if it takes place by issuing directives from management to lower levels. The other way is bottom-up improvement, when the source of improvements is the work-floor. Improvements cannot be exclusively implemented top-down or bottom-up. Top-down improvement, for instance by means of distributing a manual, will not lead to success. On the other hand, bottom-up improvement without management support in the form of time and means will not lead to the desired structural improvements. The improvement process should be supported actively by the management as well as having sufficient basis in the other sections of the organization.

- **Confine to training** It often happens that organizations pay vast sums for a training program for test personnel and then leave it at that. This is a waste of money. The knowledge gained in education should be applied in an organization that meets the minimal preconditions for improving the test process. In addition, supervision should be available during the first application of the newly learned subject matter.

- **Unbalanced improvement** The four cornerstones of a structured test approach (life-cycle model, techniques, infrastructure, and organization) must be mutually balanced. If, for example, attention is only given to test techniques or the test organization, this will lead to disappointment.

- **Unsuitable pilot** A pilot must be representative and of reasonable size and impact. On the one hand, the pilot must not provide too many risks to the primary process of the organization, but on the other hand, it should not be too free of obligations. The pilot should not confine itself to an isolated test, and the organization and the infrastructure must be emphatically involved in the test.

- **Looking upon test tools as 'the' thing** Test tools can give support in a test process. This means firstly that there must be a certain degree of *maturity* of the test process before test tools are applied, and secondly that tools can give support and no more than that. The test process cannot be done entirely by tools!

- **Structure only high-level tests** An improvement of the test process deals with all test levels and forms. It does not make any sense to purchase a super (high-level) safety net for errors made by the developers. This is far too expensive! The improvement must also be aimed at the low-level tests, because there a lot of defects can be discovered at a far lower price.

- **Underestimation of the implementation** In particular, the phase after the definition of the improvement actions is often underestimated. The 'nicest' activity, thinking how everything should be done, is over. The external experts leave because their task is done and the internal change group lowers the meeting frequency, because the organization 'only' has to implement the recommendations. These, however, are the most difficult activities of the entire process, with the highest resistance to overcome. Here, points of interest are:
  - measure the progress and the results;
  - present visible results;
  - prevent taking too large steps at once;
  - prevent the changes ending up as 'shelfware.'

- **Too many promises raise false expectations** Improving the test process costs time and goes hand in hand with ups and downs. It is important not to raise unrealistic expectations about the period in which visible results can be obtained. In the short term, small successes can be achieved; in the longer term, the advantages are more clear and visible, on the whole.

CHAPTER SEVEN

Levels by key area

In this chapter the levels of each key area are explained further and the related checkpoints and improvement suggestions are described. This chapter mainly serves as a reference.

The arrangement is as follows:

- Each level is described, clarifying the importance of that level.

- The checkpoints for that particular level are described; these have to be met to classify the test process for that level.

- Checkpoints in the form of dependencies on other levels are explained separately. An overview of these dependencies can be found in Section 7.21.

- For each level, improvement suggestions are described, giving instructions on how the *related* level can be achieved. When the test process is at the starting level and help is required in achieving level A, the improvement suggestions for level A should be followed.

7.1 Test strategy

One of the most important key areas is the test strategy. The aim of the test strategy is:

Finding the most important defects as early and as cheaply as possible

---

'Most important' is related to the risks for the organization if the system is of insufficient quality. The test strategy defines which requirements and (product) risks are covered by what tests. The better each test level defines its own strategy and the more the different test level strategies are adjusted to each other, the higher the quality of the overall test strategy.

As explained in Section 5.2.2, test process improvement usually starts with the high-level tests. As a consequence, for this key area a test process passes through the following levels of maturity: the first level starts with a risk-based test strategy for a single high-level test, then a strategy for all high-level tests is coordinated, until finally a total strategy involving all tests and evaluations is achieved.

A feature of the start level is that the test is only controlled by resources and time. Usually only one test technique is used and only the functionality is tested. Also, there is no coordination between the different test levels in the area of quality characteristics to be checked, the area of consideration of the test, and so on.

7.1.1 Strategy for single high-level test (A)

Description

The customer of a test expects certain qualities of the system to be delivered which are very different for each system. It is of great importance that you can communicate with the customer about this, and, depending on the customer's demands, translate them into a test approach.

A risk assessment forms the basis for the test strategy, because it is important for optimizing the test effort (that is, test coverage). In determining the strategy an analysis is made of what, where, and how much is to be tested to find the optimal balance between the desired quality and the amount of time/money required. An optimization takes place to distribute resources among the test activities.

EXAMPLE 7.1

Discussing the test strategy with a customer is often regarded as a revelation. Suddenly, all sorts of choices are available, instead of just those involving time and money. By defining it in more detail, the test process can be better managed. This inspires confidence in the customer and also makes negotiating time and money issues easier. When a customer wants testing to be cheaper, the test manager can present the customer with a choice: should a particular test be omitted or should another test be performed less thoroughly? This gives the customer the opportunity to defend his or her own budget. This is in contrast to well-known but embarrassing discussions such as:

Test manager	Project manager
'We need four people for four weeks.'	
	'I have three people for three weeks.'
'OK, but then we can test less.'	
	'What or how are you going to test less then?'
'We don't know yet, but if we have less time we can test less, and that involves a larger risk for the system.'	
	'How much larger is that risk then?'
etc.	

EXAMPLE 7.2

In a government department a test advisor is commissioned to audit a test project. When the strategy is examined in the test plan, at first sight it is done precisely by the book, with quality characteristics, subsystems, and test techniques. When the advisor subsequently does a spot-check on a number of worked-out test cases, he finds that the cases are not worked out according to one of the techniques, but that an informal 'home-grown' technique is used. The answers to his question concerning why the techniques have not been used is that the test plan was not really found to be workable. When he continues asking questions, the root of the problem emerges: the system to be tested is a new release, with a limited number of changes compared to the current release. The strategy has, however, been worked out as if it were a newly built system. The result is that parts that are important, but have (almost) not been changed, were still prescribed a heavy test technique. No wonder that the testers could not and did not want to work on the basis of the planned strategy.

Checkpoints

[?] A motivated consideration of the product risks takes place, for which knowledge of the system, its use and its operational management is required.

[?] There is a differentiation in test depth, depending on the risks and, if present, the acceptance criteria: not all subsystems are tested equally thoroughly and not every quality characteristic is tested (equally thoroughly).

? One or more test specification techniques are used, suited to the required depth of a test.

? For retests also, a (simple) strategy determination takes place, in which a motivated choice of variations between 'test solutions only' and 'full retest' is made.

Checkpoints: dependencies

Test specification techniques, level A, Informal techniques

Techniques are necessary to make concrete the choices for lighter or heavier testing.

Commitment and motivation, level A, Assignment of budget and time

The strategy needs to be discussed with the customer of the test, because it is strongly related to the time and money needed.

Improvement suggestions

Involve the various interested parties such as end user, systems manager, and project manager in determining the test strategy.

Create awareness by indicating the risks of the current working method, or indicate how testing can be done more cheaply and/or faster.

If there is only one specification technique at hand, then try to fit in more and/or less depth by means of simple variations. An example of more or less depth is testing or not testing boundary values. Boundary values are values close to the limit of a range. In the condition 'A $>= 10$', 9, 10, and 11 are boundary values.

For retesting, draw up a working method in which consideration of a full retest, a 'thin' retest (per defect/function/subsystem), or even no retest should be motivated (and recorded) each time.

Distinguish subsystems and quality characteristics and try to assign a relative importance to each subsystem and each quality characteristic. Translate this importance into a lighter or heavier test.

To keep the test lead time as short as possible, 'tiled' testing can be a solution. Instead of waiting for the whole system to be realized, test execution starts for each subsystem finished. Points of interest are: coordination with the developer (who has to deliver testable subsystems) and the risk of regression (an already tested subsystem suddenly does not function properly after the delivery of another subsystem).

Determine and maintain a regression test which is used to test new releases of the system for regression. Such a test is often composed of already existing test cases and is suitable for automation.

Eventually perform the complete determination of the strategy. Here is a short description of the steps that must be taken to reach a test strategy:

- **Determine quality characteristics** In consultation with the customer and any other persons involved, the quality characteristics on which the test is to be focused are determined. During the test process, the test results of the selected quality characteristics are reported to the customer.

- **Determine relative importance of quality characteristics** Based on the results of the preceding step, indicate how to distribute the test effort among the selected quality characteristics. The starting point is that the testing of each quality characteristic is equally time-consuming.

- **Break down into subsystems** In this step the IT system is broken down into subsystems. The division is in principle the same as the one that is made in the design documentation. If deviations from this division are made, they must be explicitly motivated, describing the reason. If conversion software is being developed, this software should be treated as an individual subsystem. In addition, the 'total system' is often recognized, to indicate the relative importance of a possible integral test.

- **Determine relative importance of system parts** Based on the results of the preceding step, indicate how to distribute the test effort among the subsystems. The starting point is that testing each subsystem is equally time-consuming. Next, indicate for each subsystem which quality characteristics are applicable and how heavily these should be tested, in relation to the assigned importance.

- **Determine the measuring techniques to be used** As a final step within the test strategy, measuring and in particular test specification techniques are selected which are applied to the selected quality characteristics and subsystems.

7.1.2 Combined strategy for high-level tests (B)

Description
Coordinating the test strategies of the different high-level tests prevents tests being performed twice or 'holes' appearing between the tests. Also, this provides a better possibility of performing the tests at the right moment, that is, when (with equal test coverage) the costs of testing plus the costs of reworking and retesting are at their lowest level. A condition of this coordination is that there is an insight into what is tested or not tested by each high-level test and at which depth testing takes place.

Checkpoints
- Coordination takes place between the different high-level tests, often the system, acceptance, and production acceptance tests, in the field of test strategy (risks, quality characteristics, area of consideration of the test, and planning).

[?] The result of the coordination is a coordinated strategy, which is put in writing. During the total test process, this strategy is controlled.

[?] Each high-level test determines its own test strategy, based on the coordinating strategy, as described in level A.

[?] Deviations from the coordinating strategy are reported, after which a substantiated adjustment to the coordinating strategy is made, based on the risks.

Checkpoints: dependencies

Life-cycle model, level A, Planning, Specification, Execution

For coordination, what, how, and when to test (phase planning) must be agreed beforehand. Afterwards it should be made clear that the work is done according to the agreements made. This requires insight into the process, for which a life-cycle model is a precondition.

Test specification techniques, level B, Formal techniques

Because the various tests are to be coordinated, higher demands are made on the insight into the quality and depth of each test.
This means the use of more formal test specification techniques.

Commitment and motivation, level B, Testing integrated in project organization

To realize coordination, commitment from the project management is required. This management must therefore desire to have an insight into the quality and depth of testing.

Communication, level B, Project communication (defects, change control)

Coordination requires that there is communication throughout the test process between the test levels and with the rest of the project.

Test process management, level B, Planning, execution, monitoring, and adjusting

Insight into the quality of each test means that not only can plans be trusted, but the test processes should be monitored and adjusted.

Improvement suggestions

Begin by obtaining insight into what the different tests do. Important here is the extent to which insight can be obtained into the depth and completeness of the individual tests. Indicate possible risks.

Often improvement of the test process starts with a certain test level and there is no coordination yet with other test levels. In determining the strategy of this test level, define what is expected of other tests (in the area of test coverage).

Try to find obvious 'holes' or duplicate testing and initiate a discussion about them. Make clear the importance of insight.

Appoint a test coordinator who coordinates test levels, records them in a master test plan, and also continues to monitor the coordination. The test coordinator reports to the project manager and possibly also to the customer of the system. To prevent an entanglement of interests, it is preferred that the test coordinator is independent of the various test levels.

Establishing an acquisition inspection can be considered, in which testware of a certain test level is evaluated by another party with regard to its completeness and correctness. The system test, for example, delivers to the acceptance test a functionally tested system, including test cases. The acceptance test evaluates these test cases (complete or spot-check) and performs a test case on the delivered software when in doubt. It can then direct its main effort to testing the suitability of the system for the organization and/or the usability of the system.

In the case of much overlap between certain test levels, combining them can be an option; for example, combining the system and acceptance tests into an integrated test. Points of interest are responsibilities and expectations. Legitimate reasons for the organization to prefer an integrated test are:

- the possibility offered to the users to judge the functionality thoroughly in a more suitable environment that is less subject to heavy procedures;

- the suitability of the system test environment for the, in the first instance (artificial), testing of aspects such as stress, authorization, regressiveness, etc.;

- early diagnosis and especially the correction of relatively important defects in the development process by using acceptance test cases;

- early exchange of knowledge about the IT system by developers and about the subject matter by users;

- the common use of the test environment and the related management procedures;

- the use of test tools, which normally cannot be used in the as-if-production environment for security reasons, is at the disposal of the users, including technical support;

- timely transfer of knowledge to the users and possible (future) system managers about testing and the use of test tools in particular;

- early involvement in testing will inspire users to actively help thinking about testing, thus improving the implementation and the degree of acceptance;

- the integrated test optimizes the use of resources; personnel and test facilities are deployed from one source and conflicts of priorities are prevented in time;

- placing the test under one management improves mutual understanding and communication between the parties.

EXAMPLE 7.3

For a government department a large new system is being developed. The developer is responsible for design, realization, unit test, and system test. Both users and external test experts are used for the acceptance test. When the testing of the first release of this system is being evaluated, it turns out that the system and acceptance tests show much overlap in test coverage. The system test is small and takes place in a relatively unstructured manner, whereas the acceptance test has a broader area of consideration and is much more thorough. In the acceptance test many defects are found which should have been found in the system test. As a solution to limit the overlap to a minimum, the choice has been made to combine both tests. Although the former acceptance testers for the subsequent release have been delivered, a system that in fact has a lower quality (because no system test is performed anymore), a good and fast defects procedure, extra capacity in the form of the system testers, and adequate expectation management caused the net result to be positive. Also, better understanding and communication between developers and testers has been a positive result.

7.1.3 Combined strategy for high-level tests plus low-level tests or evaluation (C)

Description

By involving the low-level tests or evaluation levels in the coordination, yet more possibilities for optimization are available.

The advantages of low-level tests are:

- they require little communication, as often the finder is also both the error producer and the person who corrects the defect;

- they find defects at an earlier stage of the system development cycle than the high-level tests.

Evaluation compared to testing means finding more in less time and earlier in the development process. However, not everything can be evaluated, which is why testing remains very important. Expanding the scope of coordination from testing to evaluation provides many extra possibilities for optimizing effort. In particular, non-functional quality characteristics such as maintainability, portability, or reliability can often be better evaluated than tested.

Involving either evaluation or low-level tests in the total test strategy is profitable to the total test process, because this creates more possibilities for optimizing the strategy, that is, finding the most important defects as early and as cheaply as possible.

Checkpoints

[?] Coordination takes place between the high-level tests and the low-level tests or the evaluation levels in the area of test strategy (risks, quality characteristics, area of consideration of the test/evaluation, and planning).

[?] The result of the coordination is a coordinated strategy, which is documented. During the total (evaluation and) test process this strategy is controlled.

[?] Each high-level test determines, on the basis of the coordination, its own test strategy, as described in level A.

[?] (if applicable) Each low-level test determines, on the basis of the coordination, its own test strategy, as described in key area Low-level testing, level C.

[?] (if applicable) Each evaluation level determines, on the basis of the coordination, its own evaluation strategy, as described in key area Evaluation, level B.

[?] Deviations from the coordinating strategy are reported, after which, on the basis of the risks, a substantiated adjustment of the coordinating strategy is made.

Checkpoints: dependencies

▨ (if applicable) Low-level testing, level C, Low-level test strategy

The low-level tests have to be able to determine and execute a test strategy within the coordinating strategy.

▨ (if applicable) Evaluation, level B, Evaluation strategy

The evaluation levels have to be able to determine and execute an evaluation strategy within the coordinated strategy.

▨ (if applicable) Moment of involvement, level C, Start of requirements definition

The total strategy must be determined at an early stage.

Improvement suggestions

Start communicating the coordinating strategy of the high-level tests to the department or people responsible for the low-level tests (= developers) or evaluations (= often quality assurance). Find overlaps and holes in total coverage between all these tests and evaluations.

Find out if it is better for certain high-level tests to be performed during low-level tests or evaluation and vice versa. The verification of norms and standards of the software (quality characteristic: maintainability) can, for example, be part of a test or an evaluation.

EXAMPLE 7.4

In the development of a new system the tests are mutually coordinated under the responsibility of a test coordinator. The system consists of a number of program types (screen, database validation, processing, and so on) which are realized by a number of building teams. For each program type it is agreed which test technique the developer should use for testing. Besides the software, a building team delivers the related test cases. These are validated for correctness and completeness by a representative of the test coordinator. If the test cases are not correct, or their number is insufficient, then that particular part of the system delivery is refused. In the beginning much is rejected, but the number of rejections decreases quickly. Also, the building teams have more certainty about the quality of the programs they deliver. In a number of cases it has turned out that using the prescribed technique is not possible, after which an alternative technique is chosen by mutual agreement.

Although this working method does not provide assurance that the developer actually executed the test cases, the subsequent tests show that the delivered programs are of a high quality on the functional level.

Both low-level tests and evaluation levels start earlier than high-level tests. In the coordination you will have to take this earlier start into account and begin on time.

Combine the inspection of the test basis (see also key area Life-cycle model, level B) with evaluation of the specifications.

Exchange testware between the different test levels, for example between the acceptance test and unit test. The advantage is that certain tests do not have to be prepared twice. Beware that the tendency not to prepare or execute one's own test can arise, so that the testware takes over the role of the specifications ('If the test cases are processed well, the program is built well').

7.1.4 Combined strategy for all test and evaluation levels (D)

Description

This description is similar to the preceding level C, only now there is coordination between high-level tests, low-level tests, and the evaluation levels, to achieve further optimization of the total test and evaluation strategy.

Checkpoints

[?] Coordination takes place between the high-level tests, the low-level tests, and the evaluation levels in the area of test strategy (risks, quality characteristics, area of consideration of the test/evaluation, and planning).

[?] The result of the coordination is a coordinating strategy, which is documented. During the total evaluation and test process this strategy is controlled.

[?] Each high-level test determines its own test strategy on the basis of the coordination, such as described for level A.

[?] Each low-level test determines its own test strategy on the basis of the coordination, such as described in the key area Low-level testing, level C.

[?] Each evaluation level determines its own evaluation strategy on the basis of the coordination, such as described in the key area Evaluation, level B.

[?] Deviations from the coordinating strategy are reported, after which a substantiated adjustment of the coordinating strategy is made on the basis of the risks.

Checkpoints: dependencies

Low-level testing, level C, Low-level test strategy

The low-level tests have to be able to determine and execute a test strategy within the coordinated strategy.

Evaluation, level B, Evaluation strategy

Evaluation has to be able to determine and execute an evaluation strategy within the coordinated strategy.

Moment of involvement, level C, Start of requirements definition

The total strategy should be determined at an early stage.

Improvement suggestions

Appoint a Test/Evaluation Coordinator (TEC) who coordinates the evaluations and tests and also continuously monitors this coordination. The TEC reports to the project manager and possibly also to the system's customer. A point of interest is the independence of the TEC.

Make the test and evaluation plan an integral part of the (system development) project plan.

7.2 Life-cycle model

Within the test process a number of phases can be distinguished, such as planning, preparation, specification, execution, and completion. Each phase consists of a number of activities; for each activity its aim, the products to be delivered, and how the activity must be performed are described. A life-cycle model makes the test process manageable, because it becomes clear who has to do what and when, and the different activities can be planned and monitored in mutual cohesion. When this knowledge is lacking, some activities are executed too late or are forgotten, while other activities cost too much time because no adjustments can be made. Also, there is no insight into progress and therefore no insight into the amount of time still required. Finally, the test process is probably on the critical path of system development for longer than necessary.

7.2.1 Planning, Specification, Execution (A)

Description
The most important phases in the test process are Planning, Specification, and Execution.

The main activity of the Planning phase is defining a test plan. A test plan defines *how*, by *whom*, *with what*, and *when* the test activities are to be executed.

The main activities of the Specification phase are defining the test cases and preparing the test execution. In addition, the realization of the infrastructure is provided.

The aim of the Execution phase is performing the specified tests to gain insight into the quality of the test object.

Checkpoints

▢ For the test (at least) the following phases are distinguished: planning, specification, and execution. These are subsequently performed, possibly per subsystem. A certain overlap between the phases is allowed.

Activities to be performed for each phase are mentioned below. Each activity is supplied with sub-activities and/or aspects. These are meant as additional information and are not obligatory.

- For the Planning phase:

Activity	Sub-activities/aspects	Product
Formulate assignment	Customer and supplier Area of consideration Aim Precondition Starting points	Defined in test plan
Determine the test basis	Determine relevant documentation Identify documentation	Defined in test plan
Determine test strategy	Strategy determination Estimating	Defined in test plan

Set up organization	Determine required functions
	Allocate tasks, authorizations,
	   and responsibilities
	Describe organization
	Allocate personnel
	Determine training
	Determine communication
	   structures
	Determine reporting lines
		Defined in test plan

Set up test deliverables	Determine test products Set up norms and standards	Defined in test plan
Define infrastructure and tools	Define test environment Define test tools Define office environment Define infrastructure planning	Defined in test plan
Set up management	Define test process management (progress, quality, reporting) Define infrastructure management Define test product management Define defects procedure	Defined in test plan
Determine planning	Set up general planning	Defined in test plan

Produce test plan	Determine risks, threats, and
	   measures
	Determine test plan
	Finalize and agree test plan
	   (customer approval)
		Test plan

- For the Specification phase:

Activity	Sub-activities/aspects	Product
Design test cases and test scripts	Test cases Define starting test databases Test scripts	Test cases Definition of starting test database Test scripts
Specify intake of test object and infrastructure	Checklist test object and infrastructure (completeness check) Test script pretest	Checked test object and infrastructure Test script pretest
Realize test infrastructure	Test environment Test tools	Operational test environment and tools

- For the Execution phase:

Activity	Sub-activities/aspects	Product
Take in test object and infrastructure	Take in infrastructure and test object (completeness check) Perform pretest	Testable test object
Set up starting test databases		Starting test databases
Execute (re)tests	Execute test scripts Execute static tests (incl. evaluation of test results and analysis of differences)	Test defects Test reports

Checkpoints: dependencies

▨ Commitment and motivation, level A, Assignment of budget and time

There must be enough commitment from the (project) management to apply a life-cycle model. In particular, the first phases, Planning and Specification, are not aimed at test execution and can therefore give the impression that they are superfluous.

Improvement suggestions

Focus attention on the test process staying on the critical path of the project for as short a time as possible. Usually testing comes onto the critical path when the developer has delivered the software for test execution. Beforehand, the test process should have dealt with as many matters as possible that do not require the presence of the software to be tested. This makes the lead time of the total project as short as possible and/or there is a maximum amount of time available to perform all planned tests.

7.2.2 Planning, Preparation, Specification, Execution, and Completion (B)

Description

With the complete life-cycle model two phases are added: preparation and completion.

The Preparation phase has an inspection of the test basis as its main activity. In such a study the test basis is inspected with regard to its testability. This study has a number of aims:

- Evaluation to see if the test basis is suitable for the chosen test specification techniques. If not, either other techniques have to be chosen or the test basis has to be adapted.

- Gain insight at an early stage into the quality of the test basis, so that in the case of insufficient quality timely measures can be taken.

- Catch as many defects as possible at an early stage, so that the specification phase is not delayed.

- Familiarize the testers with the test basis, so that the specification phase progresses faster and better.

In the Completion phase there are two core activities:

- Completing and bringing the testware up to date, in such a way that it is reusable for other test processes, for example in maintenance. This means that less effort has to be expended by these test processes.

- Evaluating the tested object and the test process to inform the customer about the quality of both and to make recommendations for future test processes.

Checkpoints

? For high-level tests the following phases are distinguished: Planning, Preparation, Specification, Execution, and Completion. The phases are executed consecutively, possibly per subsystem. A certain overlap between the phases is allowed.

Activities to be performed for each phase are mentioned below. Each activity is supplied with sub-activities and/or aspects. These are meant as additional information and are not obligatory.

- For the Preparation phase:

Activity	Sub-activities/aspects	Product
Inspection of test basis	Determine relevant documentation Define checklists for study Define documentation (study) Report on testability	Test basis defects Report testability

- For the Completion phase:

Activity	Sub-activities/aspects	Product
Evaluate test object	Determine unsolved defects and spot trends Determine risks at release Formulate advice	Release advice, defined in end report
Evaluate test process	Evaluation of test strategy Planning versus realization	Defined in end report
Formulate end report		End report
Conserve testware	Select testware to be conserved Collect and update testware Transfer testware	Testware

Checkpoints: dependencies

▨ Static test techniques, level A, Inspection of test basis

The inspection of the test basis in the Preparation phase requires use of a technique to be meaningful.

▨ Testware management, level A, Internal testware management

To be able to complete the testware afterwards, it has to be well managed during the test process.

Improvement suggestions

See directions in Static test techniques – Inspection of test basis.
See directions in Testware management – Reusable testware.

7.3 Moment of involvement

Although the actual test execution normally begins after the realization of the software, the test process can and should start much earlier. An earlier involvement of testing in the system development path helps to detect defects as soon as possible and/or as easily as possible, or even to prevent them. Better coordination between the different tests can take place and the time that the testing is on the critical path can be minimized.

A feature of the starting level is that the activity 'testing' starts just before or after the moment that the test execution should start (usually the software delivery date). Insight into the quality of the test planning, preparation, and specification is lacking.

7.3.1 Completion of test basis (A)

Description
A timely start allows the test cases to be prepared before the system is delivered for testing. At that moment testing will come onto the critical path of the project. Because the test cases only have to be executed (they have already been designed), the lead time of testing on the critical path of the total system development path is minimized.

Checkpoints
☐ The activity 'testing' starts simultaneously with or earlier than the completion of the test basis for a restricted part of the system that is to be tested separately.

(The system can be divided into several parts which are finished, built, and tested separately. The testing of the first subsystem has to start at the same time as or earlier than the completion of the test basis of that particular subsystem.)

Checkpoints: dependencies
▨ Life-cycle model, level A, Planning, Specification, Execution

Starting earlier only makes sense if this time can be used well. The phases Planning and Specification direct the activities which can be executed before the software to be tested is available.

Improvement suggestions
Make testers and the project aware of the extra-long lead time if the activity 'testing' starts at the moment at which test execution should take place. If test cases still have to be defined at that time, it is at the expense of the test quality and/or its lead time. Testing should be on the critical path for as short a time as possible.

Appoint a test manager upon completion of the test basis (preferably earlier), whose function is to start the test process.

7.3.2 Start of test basis (B)

Description

This level implies an earlier start (than level A) to provide better coordination with other test levels about who will test what and when. The coordination is after all less useful if other tests are way ahead. Other advantages are that the test preparations begin earlier and therefore defects are found earlier.

Checkpoints

? The activity 'testing' starts simultaneously with or earlier than the phase in which the test basis (often the functional specifications) is defined.

Checkpoints: dependencies

Life-cycle model, level B, Planning, Preparation, Specification, Execution, and Completion

The Preparation phase usually detects various defects in the test basis. It is important that these defects are found as fast as possible, because then the rework costs are lowest.

Improvement suggestions

Coordinate with other tests (the test coverage of the quality characteristics, but also the area of consideration of the test, for example: does the system test check the interface with the other system or not?).

Arrange that when certain parts of the test basis are completed, a timely inspection of these parts can be performed.

Appoint a test coordinator who coordinates the tests and monitors this coordination.

Consider giving other test levels insight into the specified test cases. The advantage is that other tests can make use of these test cases for early detection of defects or misunderstandings. As an example, acceptance test cases can be given to the system test. Now, the system test can see (possibly even without software) if the system will work according to these test cases. A risk is that the system test only uses these cases (which is not the intention!) so that in fact the same test is executed twice.

7.3.3 Start of requirements definition (C)

Description

The involvement of testing in the definition of requirements gives more certainty about the quality of the system. Testing can concentrate on the facts that the quality requirements are specified fully and measurably, that the acceptance criteria are determined, and that the testability of the design and software is taken into account. Creating such clarity in this phase of the system development prevents expensive discussions about requirements and criteria later.

Checkpoints
❓ The activity 'testing' starts simultaneously with or earlier than the phase in which the requirements are defined.

Checkpoints: dependencies
▨ None.

Improvement suggestions
Involve testers in formulating requirements to ensure that the requirements are concrete, measurable, and testable.

The most important condition is that the test team has enough knowledge and experience to give good substantiation to the checkpoint mentioned above. Arrange the required expertise and/or training for this.

Ensure that acceptance criteria are determined for each demand.

See also the directions for the key area Commitment and motivation, level C, Test engineering.

7.3.4 Project initiation (D)

Description
Involving testing in this phase means that from the very beginning of system development ideas on the choice of design methodology and approach are provided from a test point of view. What is the testability of the system when a certain approach or methodology is used? Will it be easy or hard to gain insight into the quality of the system? Rapid Application Development can serve as an example: will a formal acceptance test remain necessary and if so, how much time is allowed for the test and are the intended advantages of the RAD methodology still kept intact?

Checkpoints
❓ When the project is initiated, the activity 'testing' is also started.

Checkpoints: dependencies
▨ Commitment and motivation, level C, Test engineering

The involvement of testing from project initiation requires a high degree of knowledge and experience in the test team. Also, the project management must have enough trust in the capability of the testers to involve them at such an early stage.

Improvement suggestions

Involve testers in the very first phases of the development process with the assignment to look at the testability of the system (factors are, for example, which development methodology, project approach, and so on will be chosen).

The most important condition is that the test team has enough knowledge and experience to give good substantiation to the checkpoint mentioned above. Arrange the required expertise and/or training for this.

7.4 Estimating and planning

Test planning and estimating indicate which activities have to be executed when and how many resources (people) are needed. High-quality estimating and planning are very important, because these are the basis of allocating capacity. Unreliable planning and estimating frequently result either in delays because not enough resources are allocated to perform the activities in a certain time frame, or in less efficient use of resources because too many resources are allocated.

7.4.1 Substantiated estimating and planning (A)

Description

A first important step in getting control of the planning and estimating of the test effort is that the results of these activities can be substantiated. In this way, the planning and estimating are usually of a higher quality, being more reliable and more efficient in the allocation of resources. When there is a deviation, a better analysis can be made regarding whether this is an incident or whether it has a structural character. In the second case, the entire planning probably has to be revised and possibly even the method of estimating. A structured working method enables improvement.

Optimal planning and estimating are very important. When planning or budgets are not correct, this is relatively expensive: all the stops have to be pulled out to still meet the planning or estimating requirements, test activities overrun their time, or activities will be cancelled (causing more insecurity about the quality of the object to be tested).

Checkpoints

☐ The test estimating and planning can be substantiated (so not just 'we did it this way in the last project').

☐ In the test process, estimating and planning are monitored, and adjustments are made if needed.

Life-cycle model, level A, Planning, Specification, Execution

To set up reliable estimating and planning, the different activities of the test process must be distinguished. A life-cycle model is required for this.

Improvement suggestions

Gain insight into (the quality of) the method of estimating and planning (for example, by analyzing the estimating and planning of previous projects, and how reliable these were).

Try to validate estimating in a number of ways. Possible ways to estimate the effort are as follows:

- Take a percentage of the total effort, based on experiences with similar test processes (for example, functional design: 20%, technical design, realization, and unit test: 40–45%, system test 15–20%, acceptance test 20%).

- Employ standard ratios in testing, based on experiences with similar test processes (some ratios from the authors' own experience are: 10% Preparation, 40% Specification, 45% Execution including one retest, 5% Completion; execution of a retest takes only 50% of the execution of a first test, because the testware is now 'tested' and reusable). Budget the overhead at 10–20%.

- Estimate the hours of the separate activities and subsequently extrapolate these. For example, specifying test cases for one function takes four hours; there are 100 functions, so 400 hours are needed. Adding an estimate of 50 hours for other activities in the Specification phase (infrastructure!) produces a total of 450 hours. Now, further extrapolation is possible by means of the standard ratios (see item above).

- Extrapolate the results of a test pilot.

- Reduce to percentages per test level (program, integration, system, and acceptance tests).

Work out a procedure for setting up a test estimation (for example, a minimum of two rules of thumb applied).

After finishing the project, verify the estimating and the procedure and if necessary, adjust the procedure.

Agree beforehand how to deal with learning time, excess work, and waiting times.

In the planning take into account the required time for:

- transfer (from the previous phase) and installation of the test object;

- rework and retests.

In practice, a good working method for planning turns out to be to plan the entire test process globally and each time make a detailed plan for the next three to four weeks.

7.4.2 Statistically substantiated estimating and planning (B)

Description

Metrics can be analyzed. Based on this analysis, the working method of planning and estimating can be optimized further.

Checkpoints

❓ Metrics concerning progress and quality are structurally maintained (on level B of the key area Metrics) for multiple, comparable projects.

❓ This data is used to substantiate test estimating and planning.

Checkpoints: dependencies

▨ Reporting, level B, Progress (status of tests and products), activities (costs and time, milestones), defects with priorities

Statistically substantiated estimating and planning are not useful if no progress reporting is done throughout the project.

Improvement suggestions

Arrange that each project indicates in general terms its progress and quality (defects) in reporting. Later more detail is applied, guided from the line organization. A point of interest is the growth in functionality compared to the initial planning: often the functionality of a system increases notably during the building and test phases. This is often visible in the form of a continuous flow of change suggestions.

Let the line department for testing manage and periodically analyze these metrics, looking for costs/profit index numbers. Which systems gave many problems in production, which systems fewer? What is the relationship between the index numbers and the tests performed, the development method applied, and so on? Ensure that on the basis of the above-mentioned information, improvement measures are proposed and implemented.

7.5 Test specification techniques

The following definition is used:

A test specification technique is a standardized way of deriving test cases from source information.

- a substantiated interpretation of the test strategy can be made, that is, the right coverage in the right place;

- defects can be detected in a far more effective way than random identification of test cases;

- insight into the quality and depth of the tests is given;

- tests are more reusable.

7.5.1 Informal techniques (A)

Description
The use of informal techniques means that the person writing the test specification has a lot of freedom in inventing test cases. This causes the test quality to be highly dependent on the (subject matter) skills of the person writing the specification and blurs the level of coverage compared to the test basis. However, this is far better than each tester thinking up test cases for themselves, without worrying about the documentation of these test cases.

Making predictions in the specifications of the test cases is very important, because the judging of test results afterwards under the pressure of time is often insufficiently thorough ('the result is 990; I expected something between 800 and 1000 so that number is probably correct').

Checkpoints

[?] The test cases are specified by means of a described technique.

[?] The technique requires at least a description of: (a) the starting situation, (b) the change process = test actions to be performed, and (c) the expected end result.

Checkpoints: dependencies

None

Improvement suggestions
Make testers aware of the importance of predictions.

Describe the specification technique. Try to include as many practical instructions as possible, so that the person writing the specification has somewhat restricted room for maneuver. The test cases should be described in such detail that someone other than the test case author has enough information to execute these cases.

7.5.2 Formal techniques (B)

Description

The use of formal test specification techniques has several advantages:

- A more substantiated judgment is possible about the depth and the completeness of the test.

- The testware becomes more reusable.

- The test process becomes less dependent on the author and executor of the test cases.

- The test process is more manageable because an estimate can be made in advance of how many test cases are needed. This allows for better planning and progress monitoring.

Introducing several techniques is important because different (parts of the) systems require different levels of thoroughness of testing.

Checkpoints

? Besides informal techniques, formal techniques are also used, providing unambiguous ways of getting from the test basis to test cases.

? A substantiated judgment is possible about the level of coverage of the collection of test cases (compared to the test basis).

? The testware is reusable (within the test team) by means of a uniform working method.

Checkpoints: dependencies

Test functions and training, level A, Test manager and testers

The testers need to know how to use the formal techniques. For this, training and experience are required.

Testware management, level A, Internal testware management

The use of (relatively expensive) formal techniques produces test cases. It is of the utmost importance that these test cases are reusable, either in retests or for testing later system releases. Good management of these test cases is necessary to achieve this.

Improvement suggestions

Arrange training and coaching for the testers who will work with these techniques.

Have the technique described, when it deviates from a standard technique.

Most test techniques are described in the literature (Beizer, 1990; Kaner *et al.*, 1993; Kit, 1995; Pol *et al.*, 1995), so you don't have to reinvent the wheel.

7.6 Static test techniques

Dynamic testing is the execution of test cases on running software. This is not always possible or desired. When testing is not done with working software, we speak of static testing. This form of testing concerns the evaluation of products such as documentation, procedures, sources, and so on, and is focused more on the evaluation of the measures to achieve a certain quality than the actual quality itself. An example of this is a static test of security measures. Measures can be the use of login procedures and certain database settings. Evaluating whether these measures are sufficient and in effect is static testing. If we are actually trying to break through the security, we are testing dynamically. Several quality characteristics can be statically tested (for example, reliability, maintainability, installability, portability, security). In general, static testing is cheaper and can be used earlier than dynamic testing. Here, checklists are very useful tools.

7.6.1 Inspection of test basis (A)

Description
As already described in the application of the full life-cycle model, performing an inspection of the test basis in the Preparation phase is important for three reasons: to check testability, to find early defects in the test basis, and to get to know the test basis. A technique in the form of a checklist is necessary to perform the study in a structured way, so that the important items are looked at. Otherwise, there is no insight into what has to be noticed and there is a risk that the document is merely checked for spelling.

Checkpoints
- ? Preceding the definition of the test cases, a study of the testability of the test basis is performed.
- ? In this study checklists are used.

Checkpoints: dependencies
- None

Improvement suggestions
Make testers aware of the importance of an inspection of the test basis and of the use of checklists.

Make checklists for:

- **General evaluation** This checklist contains general evaluations to be performed on the test basis, such as 'Does the table of contents match the rest of the test basis?', 'Does a logical data model exist?', 'Do screen and list layouts exist?', and so on.

- **Each test specification technique used** Not every test specification technique is suitable for a given test basis. A technique can only be used if the test basis conforms to certain requirements, specific to that technique, such as the existence of screen-prints or a data model. Describing the requirements in checklists enables a fast check on the suitability of the test basis for the chosen test technique.

Make the results of the study (defects, insight into the quality of the test basis) available to the testers and also point out that understanding and knowledge of the test basis are acquired as a result of this activity.

7.6.2 Checklists (B)

Description
Besides applying them to the inspection of the test basis, checklists can also be used for other static tests. The use of checklists makes it possible to perform these tests in a structural manner so that the focus is on important items. This gives an insight into these items of inspection. Another advantage of the use of checklists is that coordination is possible beforehand on the items to be tested. A possible difference in insight is quickly recognized.

Checkpoints
☑ Static tests other than the inspection of the test basis take place by means of checklists (approved by project and/or customer).

Checkpoints: dependencies
▨ None

Improvement suggestions
Make testers aware of the objectivity and relative completeness of checklists as means of substantiating a judgment (compared to just indicating 'the system is not easily understandable').

Make testers aware of the importance of communicating checklists beforehand to the developers and other project members, to avoid later discussions or to have a stronger position in these discussions.

Arrange that the right (subject matter or system) knowledge is available for specifying and/or performing static tests.

7.7 Metrics

Metrics are quantified observations of the characteristics of a product or process, for example the number of lines of code. Some metrics are computed from other metrics. For the test process, metrics about the progress of the process and the quality of the tested system are of vital importance. They are used to manage the test process, to substantiate the test advice, and also to compare systems or processes. Why does one system have far fewer failures in production than another, or why is one test process faster and more thorough than another? Metrics are specifically important for improving the test process to assess the consequences of certain improvement measures, by comparing data before and after the implementation of the measure.

There are two approaches to acquiring metrics: top-down and bottom-up.

In the top-down approach the wishes and requirements of higher management are the starting point. A well-known form is Basili's Goal-Question-Metric approach, in which goals are defined, based on these requirements and wishes. Questions are formulated to view to what extent the goals are met, after which metrics are identified to answer the questions. The ami method (Pulford *et al.*, 1995) provides a guide to implementing such a metrics program.

A disadvantage of a top-down approach is that management is not always aware (or agrees on) what the right targets are, because reliable information is often lacking: a chicken-and-egg problem. Also, the people on the work-floor are not always enthusiastic about cooperating, in view of the risk that their performances might be judged in the wrong way. Finally, there is a chance that the measurements may be manipulated to achieve the set targets.

In a bottom-up approach (Hetzel, 1993), the (intermediate) products, the working method used, and the people involved are regarded as a basis for the measurements. A base set of measures is proposed for each (intermediate) product:

Input: information about the resources used (people, computers, tools, other products, …) and the process steps or activities performed;

Output: information about the products to be delivered;

Result: information about the use and effectiveness of the delivered products compared to the set requirements.

The most important argument for the bottom-up approach is that the information thus acquired suffices to answer almost any question and as such helps to determine the targets. The approach is also very much focused on (the advantage for) the people carrying out the work.

In both approaches the commitment of the management is a necessary prerequisite.

Without damaging the top-down approach, it is decided to work out this key area using the bottom-up approach. This approach builds on certain base data. Each organization has, to a certain extent, its own standards and procedures for monitoring this base data. These are the elementary building blocks for each attempt to implement the use of metrics:

- Progress monitoring – estimating and monitoring resource usage, activities, products to be delivered, milestones.

- Configuration management – monitoring and managing versions and changes (source code and design documentation).

- Defects and change management – monitoring and managing defects and change proposals.

We indicate below what the measurements refer to for each level.

7.7.1 Project metrics (product) (A)

Description

For the test process, metrics concerning the progress of the process and the quality of the tested system are of great importance. They are used for managing the test process, to substantiate the test advice, and also to compare systems or processes. This level consists of metrics for Input and Output.

Checkpoints

[?] In the (test) project Input metrics are recorded:
- used resources – hours;
- performed activities – hours and lead time (duration);
- size and complexity of the tested system – in function points, number of functions, and/or building effort.

[?] In the (test) project Output metrics are recorded:
- test products – specifications and test cases, log reports;
- test progress – performed tests, status (finished/not finished);
- number of defects – defects by test level, by subsystem, by cause, priority, status (new, in solution, corrected, retested).

[?] The metrics are used in test reporting.

Checkpoints: dependencies

[■] Commitment and motivation, level B, Testing integrated in project organization

Recording metrics should be regarded as an investment in the quality of the test process. This requires a certain level of quality thinking by the customers of the test.

▨ Test process management, level B, Planning, execution, monitoring, and adjustment

The figures used for metrics must be reliable. This requires good management of the test process.

▨ Reporting, level B, Progress (status of tests and products), activities (costs and time, milestones), defects with priorities

Recording metrics is of little use if metrics are not reported and used.

▨ Defect management, level A, Internal defect management

An important part of the metrics is the defects. Good management of these is a necessity.

Improvement suggestions
Begin on a small scale: record the hours and lead time for the phases and the number of defects per phase.

Start measuring as early as possible, preferably even before the start of the improvement process, so that later there will be comparison material.

In good defect administration, this measuring can be expanded continuously.

Arrange that the organization (and not each project separately) is involved in determining the metrics to be recorded.

The implementation of metrics is often regarded as a separate project because of the impact it has on the organization. Bear this in mind and do not underestimate the problems. There is much literature available on this subject.

Never use metrics to check people on an individual basis, for example their productivity. The danger of incorrect interpretation is too great. Also, it could lead to the manipulation of data.

Make the metrics a permanent part of the templates for (end) reporting and for test plans (for substantiating test estimating).

EXAMPLE 7.5

We want to appraise testers on their productivity and to do this on the basis of the number of finished test cases per time unit. It turns out that tester 1 produces significantly fewer test cases per time unit than tester 2. The reason for this, however, is that tester 1 is the better tester of the two and therefore has to specify the most complex tests!

7.7.2 Project metrics (process) (B)

Description

Besides the Input and Output metrics of the preceding level, in this level the Result metrics are also looked at: how well do we test anyway? Just going by the number of defects found does not tell us much about this: if many defects are found, it does not always mean that the test was good; development might have been badly done. On the other hand, few defects found might mean that the system has been built well, but might also mean that the testing has been insufficient.

Metric information is useful for substantiating advice about the quality of the tested object and can also serve as input in the improvement of the test process. When the test process has been improved, you should also be able to check this in one way or another. Metrics help to visualize the results of improvements.

Checkpoints

▨ In the (test) project Result measurements are made for at least two of the items mentioned below:
- defect find-effectiveness:
    - the defects found compared to the total defects present (in %); the last entity is difficult to measure, but think of the number of defects found in later tests or in the first months of production;
    - analyze which previous test should have found the defects (this indicates something about the effectiveness of the preceding tests!);
- defect find-efficiency:
    - the number of defects found per hour spent, measured over the entire test period or over several test periods;
- test coverage level:
    - the test targets covered by a test case compared to the number of possible test targets (in %). These targets can be determined for functional specifications as well as for the software; think, for example, of statement or condition coverage;
- testware defects:
    - the number of 'defects' found whose cause turned out to be wrong testing, compared to the total number of defects found (in %);
- perception of quality:
    - by means of reviews and interviews of users, testers, and other people involved.

▨ Metrics are used in test reporting.

- Reporting, level C, Risks and recommendations, substantiated with metrics

  Recording metrics for the test process is not useful if the metrics cannot be reported and used. In level C of Reporting such metrics can be used.

- Defect management, level B, Extensive defect management with flexible reporting facilities

  Comprehensive defect administration is needed to provide for the collection of metrics about the quality of the test process.

Improvement suggestions
Tools often provide good support in collecting metrics.

7.7.3 System metrics (C)

Description
The functioning of a system in production is in fact the final test. Expanding metrics to cover the entire system instead of just the development phase gives a much higher quality of information acquired. The metric information from the development phase can in fact give a very positive image of the system quality, but when subsequently a massive amount of failures occur in production, this should be taken into account in making a judgment.

Checkpoints
- ? The metrics mentioned above are recorded for development, maintenance, and production.

- ? Metrics are used in the assessment of the effectiveness and efficiency of the test process.

Checkpoints: dependencies
- Scope of methodology, level B, Organization generic

  Managing metrics for a system requires that the data delivered from the various phases is mutually compatible. A generic test methodology is a precondition for this.

- Communication, level C, Communication within the organization about the quality of the test processes

  The final aim of collecting metrics for systems is achieving improvement of the (test) processes. Metrics should be discussed in a coordinated meeting.

▧ Test process management, level C, Monitoring and adjustment in the organization

The data required for metrics comes from different processes. The reliability of this data is of great importance. This requires management at the organization level.

Improvement suggestions

Begin as soon as possible with the registering of defect find-effectiveness (number of defects in test/number of defects in production) and defect find-efficiency (number of defects in test/number of test hours). These figures can be compared for each project and/or system.

Arrange that the line department for testing and/or the maintenance organization manages metrics centrally. Each project transfers its accumulated metrics to this line department.

The maintenance organization and/or line department assesses the effectiveness and efficiency of test processes.

7.7.4 Organization metrics (>1 system) (D)

Description

The quality of one system is higher than the quality of another. By making use of mutually comparable metrics, better systems can be recognized and the differences analyzed. These results can be used for further process improvement.

Checkpoints

❓ Organization-wide mutually comparable metrics are maintained for the already mentioned data.

❓ Metrics are used in assessing the effectiveness and efficiency of the separate test processes, to achieve an optimization of the generic test methodology and future test processes.

Checkpoints: dependencies

▧ None.

Improvement suggestions

The line or staff department responsible for testing demands uniform metrics from the different projects.

Each project or the maintenance organization transfers the accumulated metrics to this department.

7.8 Test tools

Before dealing with the key area test tools, it is important first to define what is meant by a test tool:

A test tool is an automated means which supports one or more test activities, such as planning and control, specification, setting up starting test databases, test execution and analysis.

Here, the emphasis is on *support*. Or, higher productivity and/or efficiency must be achieved when using the test tool. This means that a test tool is only a tool when it brings profit; using a tool should not be an aim in itself.

Automation within the test process can take place in very different ways and generally has one or more of the following aims:

- Fewer hours needed

- Shorter lead time

- More test depth

- Greater flexibility in testing

- More/faster insight into the status of the test process

- Better motivation of the test personnel

7.8.1 Planning and control tools (A)

Description
Planning and control tools may support the following activities:

- Budgeting

- Planning

- Progress control

- Configuration management

- Defect administration

Many of these tools are not specifically for testing, but for project management in general. The tools are relatively cheap, easy to implement, require little learning time, and enhance the quality and speed of the processes concerned.

Checkpoints

[?] Automated tools (other than standard word processing) are used for the defect administration and for at least two other activities of Planning and control.

Checkpoints: dependencies

[ ] None.

Improvement suggestions

Preferably use existing tools in the organization, if they meet the needs.

7.8.2 Execution and analysis tools (B)

Description

Test execution and analysis can be supported by several sorts of tools:

- Capture & Playback

- Load & Stress

- Test coverage

- Test data generator

- Simulators

- Drivers and stubs

- Compiler

- Comparator

- Static analyzer

- Query languages

- Debugger

- Monitor

In Appendix C you will find a short description of each of these tools.

These tools usually have higher costs (in terms of purchasing, training, implementation, use) than the tools for planning and control, but on the other hand the potential profits in terms of quality, money, and/or time are also greater. The most important reason to rank the use of these tools one level higher is that the failure risk with these tools is relatively large. Failure in this context is a situation in which the profits will never exceed the costs.

EXAMPLE 7.6

In a large financial organization a Capture & Playback tool is deployed to automate a test which is to be executed frequently. From the start of the implementation of the tool much attention has been given to good maintainability of the automated test scripts. This maintainability has been achieved on the one hand by setting up the structure of the automated scripts in a modular way and on the other by preserving the test data separate from the tool scripts.

Although at first this meant more work and also required programming expertise, the advantages became evident further down the line. Adjustments in the system could be processed in the automated test scripts with minimal effort, therefore re-executing the scripts was faster than could have been done manually.

It is possible that an investigation was done concerning the application of tools for a test process, but the conclusion was that application was not justified. Despite the fact that this is a very 'mature' working method, it means that the test process does not meet this level.

Checkpoints

? At least two sorts of automated tools are used for test execution, such as Capture & Playback tools, test coverage tools, etc.

? The test team has a general insight into the cost/profit ratio of these tools.

Checkpoints: dependencies

Test functions and training, level A, Test managers, testers

A good use of test tools for execution and of analysis tools requires expertise from the test personnel.

Test specification techniques, level B, Formal techniques

(Only applicable if Capture & Playback or coverage tools are used.) Automated test execution is only useful if the test scripts are easily maintainable. This implies the use of test specification techniques. Also, the use of coverage tools (which percentage of the system has been covered with test cases) implies these techniques, because without techniques it is nearly impossible to acquire the desired coverage.

Improvement suggestions

List and substantiate the needs and the necessity for using tools. Do not limit this investigation to commercially available packages only. Very small, home-made tools such as stubs, drivers, displays in the system, and so on can be very useful. The developer can often make these tools in a short time.

Execute a structured selection and implementation process. Requirements (restrictions) and wishes are possible for different aspects:

- functionality (for example, programmable, recognition of GUI objects, etc.);
- service level;
- quality;
- costs;
- (environment) hardware and software (very important: does the tool work in a specific environment?);
- number of users, knowledge level, quality documentation.

Arrange training and support for a tool to be purchased.
Execute a pilot.
See the critical factors for Capture & Playback test tools in Appendix C.
Provide tool expertise in the team (often someone with technical and programming knowledge).
Make a description of how the setup of the tool should be done.
Make a substantiated cost/profit consideration before purchasing the tool. To get an impression of the differences between manual (M) and automated testing by means of a Capture & Playback tool (A), read the following.

1 **Find out which test effort qualifies for automation** Suppose that a regression test is executed four times a year, in which four persons work full-time for three weeks: $4 \times 4 \times 3 \times 5 = 240$ person-days a year.

2 **Estimate the 'pure execution time'; this is the time that can be automated** The 'pure execution time' is the actual time that a person needs to perform test cases on the application, plus the time spent on detecting differences (calculation produces 10 instead of 9). *Not* included in 'pure execution time' is the analysis of the differences and detection of the cause (the calculation produces 10 instead of 9 because in function X a certain percentage is not taken into account).

In the example of 240 person-days a year, we estimate the 'pure execution time' to be a quarter, so 60 person-days a year.

3 **Make estimates for the following propositions**
- Automated handling of the first test execution costs on average X times as much as a manual first test execution (in the example we use $X = 2$, so $A = M \times 2$).
- Automated retesting is Y times faster than manually (in the example we use $Y = 4$, $A = M/4$).

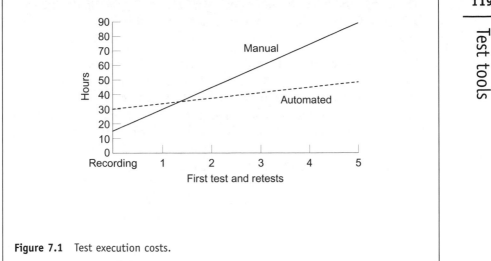

Figure 7.1 Test execution costs.

4 **Calculate the possible gain in time**
   - Manual = 60 person-days a year, or 15 person-days for each regression test.
   - Automated = (first test costs twice as much: 15 × 2) + (retests are four times faster: 3 × 15/4) = 41 person-days in the first year and (4 × 15/4) = 15 person-days each following year.
   - Profits = the difference, that is, 19 person-days in the first year and 45 person-days each following year.

   The above-mentioned information can also be shown in a chart (Figure 7.1), for example to determine the break-even point, or to work out how many retests it takes for the tool to earn back its own costs.

5 **Estimate the following factors**: (where '−'stands for the costs and '+' stands for the profits of a tool)

   - − purchase of tool;
   - − training;
     set up tool;
   - − maintain scripts when changes are made (maintaining automated scripts is more labor-intensive than maintaining manual scripts);
   - + higher quality of automated test (assuming that the human tester in the execution of the Xth regression test is less observant);
   - + higher motivation and productivity of the personnel (a tool gives testing a new dimension, often it is 'fun');
   - + faster lead time.

These factors have to be estimated, in which the maintenance of automated scripts especially can cost much effort, but is also hard to predict.

6 **Now make the full cost/profit comparison** The comparison is necessarily full of assumptions, but gives a basis to reason from. It often turns out that the expectations are far too high. In any event the comparison can also be made for 'normal' tests, instead of a regression test. In that case, keep in mind that the first test execution usually takes twice as long as a retest and that not all tests will cause a retest to be done.

Check the costs and profits periodically, to see if the earn-back time has already been reached. For this, budget costs such as the setup of the tool and training separately, and include a certain overhead for the use of the tool or, on the contrary, a time profit from its use.

7.8.3 Extensive automation of the test process (C)

Description
Integration of the tools used in the different phases of the test process gives higher quality with less effort. In addition to the tools already discussed for the planning and execution phases, the preparation and specification phases can also be supported by tools:

- Case tool analyzer
- Test design

Checkpoints
[?] Automated tools (other than standard word processing) are used for the planning phase (for the activities estimating, planning, progress monitoring, configuration management, and defect administration), preparation, specification, and execution (in total at least five sorts of tool should be used).

[?] The test team has an insight into the cost/profit ratio of these tools.

Checkpoints: dependencies
None.

Improvement suggestions
Provide maximum integration of the tools. Make integration facilities a more important factor in the tool selection process.

See also the directions for tools for execution and analysis tools.

7.9 Test environment

The test execution takes place in a test environment. The main components of this environment are:

- hardware;
- software;
- communication means;
- facilities for building and using test files and databases;
- procedures.

The environment must be composed and organized in such a way that on the basis of the test results it can optimally be determined to what extent the test object meets the requirements. The environment has a large influence on the quality, lead time, and costs of the test process. Important aspects of the environment are responsibilities, management, timely and sufficient availability, representativeness, and flexibility.

7.9.1 Managed and controlled test environment (A)

Description
Testing should take place in a controlled environment. Often the environment is therefore separated from the development or production environment. Controlled means among other things that the test team owns the environment and that nothing can be changed without the permission of the test team. This reduces the chance of disturbance by other activities. Examples of disturbances are: software deliveries that are installed without the knowledge of the test team or changes in the infrastructure that lead to the situation where the test environment is no longer linked to the development or the production environment.

The more the test environment resembles the final production environment, the more certainty there is that later in the production no problems will arise which are caused by a deviant environment. In the testing of time-behavior in particular, a representative environment is of high importance.

The environment should be organized in such a way that test execution can take place as efficiently as possible. An example of this is the presence of sufficient test databases, so that the testers do not have to wait for each other.

Checkpoints
? Only with the permission of the test manager can changes and/or deliveries take place in the test environment.

▢ The environment must be set up in time.

▢ The test environment is managed (with regard to setup, availability, maintenance, version management, error handling, authorizations, …).

▢ The saving and restoring of certain test situations can be arranged quickly and easily.

▢ The environment is sufficiently representative for the test to be performed, which means: the closer the test level is to production, the more the environment is 'as-if-production.'

Checkpoints: dependencies

▨ Test functions and training level A, Test manager, testers

Good management of the test environment requires skilled test personnel.

Improvement suggestions

If there is not enough awareness in the rest of the project, collect examples in which the test environment was 'uncontrolled' and communicate the problems that were caused by this.

Take measures concerning restrictive factors that cannot be changed (for example, when the lead time of the transfer of a delivery is always at least one week, restrict the number of (re-)deliveries by performing extra test work in the other environments or preceding test levels).

Make sure that the responsibility for the environment rests with the test manager.

Arrange for aspects such as the backup and restore of test situations, management, required tools (query languages!), the number of required test databases, and so on to be available in time.

A well-known test problem is that tests executed in the same environment disturb each other:

EXAMPLE 7.7

Tester 1 enters some customer data, then wants to check it but cannot find any customers. The reason for this is that tester 2 has checked the clean-up functionality and deleted all the customers.

The system date is also notorious in this respect. Some calculations rely strongly on this. When another tester changes the system date for his or her own test, calculations will give unexpected results.

To circumvent this problem and also decrease the lead time, consider organizing multiple test environments or databases. Testers can then work simultaneously without having to consider each other's tests. A disadvantage is that the management of the test environments becomes more complex.

Also, shifts can be set up to overcome this (for example, team 1 performs tests in the morning, team 2 performs tests in the afternoon).

Ensure that technical knowledge is available to the test team.

Obtain insight into what is representative (this is often more difficult than it seems at first sight) in terms of database sizing, parametrizing, contents, and other variations. Take into account the fact that each test level needs another representative environment (a system test, for example, is 'laboratory,' an acceptance test 'as-if-production').

Set up the environment and indicate the risks and possible measures in case of deviations.

7.9.2 Testing in the most suitable environment (B)

Description

The level of control over the different test environments is sufficiently high, which makes it easier to deviate from a 'specific' environment per test level. This makes it possible either to test in another environment (for example, execution of a part of the acceptance test in the system test environment) or to adapt the own environment quickly. The advantage of testing in another environment is either that this environment is better suited (for example, a shorter lead time or better facilities for viewing intermediate results) or that a certain test can be executed earlier. There is a conscious balancing between acquiring test results sooner and a decrease in representativeness.

Checkpoints

? Each test is performed in the most suitable environment, either by execution in another environment or by quickly and easily adapting the own environment.

? The environment is finished in time for the test and there is no disturbance by other activities during the test.

? The risks taken are analyzed and adequate measures taken.

Checkpoints: dependencies

Test strategy, level B, Combined strategy for high-level tests.

The possibility of testing in another environment requires good coordination between the different test levels. This means that a coordinated test strategy is a precondition.

Improvement suggestions

Make the testing start as soon as possible; consider on the one hand the advantages of a separate, controlled and representative environment and on the other the advantages of early testing and/or efficient test execution.

> **EXAMPLE 7.8**
>
> Parts of the production acceptance test can be executed in the system test environment, for example checks on memory usage. Also, a number of important acceptance test cases can be executed in the system test or development environment, or checks for usability can take place in the development environment.

Consider this in determining the test strategy; for example, testing starts in an earlier environment, but a final test still takes place in the own environment.

Coordinate the use of an(other) environment in time.

7.9.3 'Environment on call' (C)

Description

The test team indicates which tests it performs when and which conditions the environment must meet. The selected environment is organized and delivered in time, and the chance of external disturbances is minimal. Possible changes in the environment can be done quickly and flexibly.

Checkpoints

? The environment that is most suited for a test is very flexible and can quickly be adapted to changing requirements.

Checkpoints: dependencies

None.

Improvement suggestions

Take care that the different environments are managed well.

This level in fact demands more of the system management department than of the test process. Keep this in mind.

7.10 Office environment

The test personnel need rooms, desks, chairs, PCs, word-processing facilities, printers, telephones, and so on.

7.10.1 Adequate and timely office environment (A)

Description

Good and timely arrangement of the office infrastructure minimizes all kinds of efficiency losses such as waiting time and non-productive hours. A good arrangement of the environment also has a positive influence on the quality of the test process. One aspect is the quality of both internal and external communication and another the motivation and productivity of the people.

Checkpoints

☑ The office infrastructure needed for testing (offices, meeting rooms, telephones, PCs, network connections, office software, printers, and so on) is arranged on time.

☑ Things related to office organization have a minimal impact on the progress of the test process (as little moving as possible, physical distance between testers and the rest of the project not too large, and so on).

Checkpoints: dependencies

▨ None.

Improvement suggestions

Get information at an early stage about the delivery times of supplies.

Ensure that office moves and suchlike are budgeted separately.

If testers are located at a considerable physical distance, extra overhead hours may need to be budgeted. This shows more clearly the disadvantages of the chosen office infrastructure.

7.11 Commitment and motivation

The commitment and motivation of the people involved in testing are important prerequisites for a smoothly running test process. Those involved are not only the testers themselves but also, for example, the project management and line management. The last mentioned are especially important in creating good conditions, so that the test process receives enough time, money, and means (quantitative and qualitative) to perform a good test, in which cooperation and communication with the rest of the project give the overall process maximum efficiency.

A feature of the starting level is that testing is regarded as a necessary evil. The test team consists largely of people who are assigned to work in the test team on a part-time basis and who come from other disciplines (users, developers). Testing has a low 'status' and is seen as superfluous and/or inefficient. The overall motivation of the testers is low. Much is tested 'pro forma' and there is an overdose of confidence in the developers and designers. Defects found by testers are not dealt with structurally.

7.11.1 Assignment of budget and time (A)

Description

On this level higher and middle management are aware of the importance of testing and that testing is a considerable effort which is necessary.

It is of vital importance to raise the motivation of personnel to a sufficiently high level, because this has a direct consequence for productivity. A process can be organized very well, but without the proper motivation of personnel the total result is zero. Because motivation is a concept that almost cannot be measured, checkpoints have been set up in the form of various aspects that play a role in motivation.

Checkpoints

? Testing is regarded by personnel involved as necessary and important.

? An amount of time and budget is allocated to testing.

? Management controls testing based on time and money. A feature is that if the test time or budget is exceeded, initially a solution is sought within the testing (doing overtime or employing extra people when exceeding time limits or on the contrary cutting time and/or budget).

? In the team there is enough knowledge and experience in the field of testing.

? There are function descriptions of the various test functions within the test team.

? The activities for testing are full-time for most participants (therefore there are not many conflicts with other activities).

? There is a good relationship between the testers and other disciplines in the project and the organization.

Checkpoints: dependencies

None.

Improvement suggestions

Take stock of the problems in production or in the later tests (such as the acceptance test): what is the consequence of insufficient testing and what are the (organization) costs of detecting and correcting problems in production?

Find out what defects could have been found earlier.

Give presentations, courses, and so on to gain awareness.

Try to achieve the full-time dedication of the people assigned to testing.

Arrange training in the field of testing, but also in the fields of social skills, system development, subject matter, and so on.

Work as soon as possible with a life-cycle model and planning of testing. This is a way to optimize effort and avoid conflicts with the project and line management, because the required effort is known at an early stage.

7.11.2 Testing integrated in project organization (B)

Description

A professionally organized test process is more manageable and predictable. In case of possible overrunning (in terms of time or money), there is better insight into the cause, so that measures can be taken. Also, there is better communication between testers and other parties involved in the development path, improving the parties' coordination in planning. This way, the total process can be more efficiently organized.

Because the productivity of the people has a one-to-one relationship with motivation, it is important to keep motivation as high as possible. One way to achieve this is by a well-managed test process, as described above, so that people have more insight into the current state of affairs. Insecurity about this often reduces motivation. Other motivating factors are that other parties regard testing as very useful and that testers are offered a career path.

EXAMPLE 7.9

Although in a large organization a very substantial number of people are constantly employed in test processes, there are no functions, responsibilities, or career paths defined for these tasks on an organization level. This causes everyone to regard test work as a temporary sidestep or even as an interruption of their planned career path in system development. Even people who find testing fascinating and are good at it feel themselves compelled to perform other activities from a career point of view. An important issue in improving the test process is to include the test functions in the existing function structure with proportional reward and growth possibilities. This prevents the most experienced people leaving the test profession.

Checkpoints

- [?] All those involved find that testing has a noticeable positive influence on the quality of the product.

- [?] The management wants to have insight into the depth and quality of testing.

- [?] The management controls testing based on time, money, and quality. A feature is that the solution to test problems (for example, exceeding test time or budget) is also sought outside the test project. Possibly the developer is addressed here.

☐ In the project planning, the cycle of testing, rework, and retesting is taken into account.

☐ Testing has a say in the delivery sequence of the developer.

☐ The advice from testing is discussed in project meetings.

Checkpoints: dependencies

▨ Life-cycle model, level A, Planning, Specification, Execution

▨ Test process management, level B, Planning, execution, monitoring, and adjusting

Good integration of testing and the project means that the test process can be well planned and managed. A prerequisite for this is that the process has a phase model and is well controlled.

▨ Reporting, level B, Progress (status of tests and products), activities (costs and time, milestones), defects with priorities

▨ Defect management, level A, Internal defect management

A minimal precondition for the integration of testing in the project is that the progress and defects are well managed and reported.

Improvement suggestions

Ensure that the test manager takes part in project communication.

Arrange structural communication and coordination with the developers, which gives an insight into each other's progress.

Create an active attitude in the test team: a signaling function. Testers should work on active and timely reporting of potential quality problems.

EXAMPLE 7.10

In a project strict planning is applied. The agreement is that the developer must finish an activity on a certain date, and testing should start on the following day. However, it quickly turns out that the developer does in fact finish on that date, but the next day the software is transferred to the test environment and must be installed there. Allowing for the wide variety of problems that arise, this transfer takes two to three days each time, during which the testing cannot start. Because the planning is very strict, the test team overruns the planning by a couple of days every time. Although in the project meetings the developer and tester blame each other for this in the first instance, it is agreed that the planning must be adapted. From that time onward, two days are allocated for the transfer and the problems are largely over.

Introduce an internal test team meeting, in which the team is informed about progress, the (test) results, and the ups and downs of the project.

Figure 7.2 Motivation.

Stimulate the formation of a staff line department for testing (Figure 7.2), where the knowledge and skills of the various test teams are collected and bundled.

Give presentations and so on to make the organization and/or the project aware of the importance of testing.

7.11.3 Test engineering (C)

Description
On this level motivation, knowledge, and skills in the test team are on such a level that the test process is regarded as an essential factor in the total system development, which has to be involved in the total path at an early stage. Testing is seen not merely as a detective measure but also as a preventive measure (Figure 7.3).

The systems to be developed or maintained become more and more complex and show an increasing degree of integration. This causes great stress on the systems' testability. By taking testability into account in design and realization, it can be strongly increased, so that testing can offer more certainty about the quality of the system with less effort (Figure 7.4). An example that demonstrates insufficient testability is the problems concerning the year 2000. One of the greatest challenges is the testing of often aged and badly documented systems, which are interconnected in all kinds of ways.

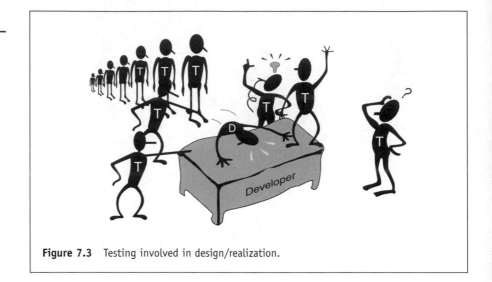

Figure 7.3 Testing involved in design/realization.

When the test process is an integral and optimized part of the development process, any lack of quality is detected (or even prevented) as early as possible in the total process, at minimal costs. This increases control over the total development process.

An optimal test process requires highly motivated and trained people. Besides internal measures to get high motivation from people, various external factors also play a role. In a well-organized development process, factors such as time, money, and quality are controlled. This prevents plans repeatedly not being met or products such as functional specifications and software being of insufficient quality. When the test team is confronted with

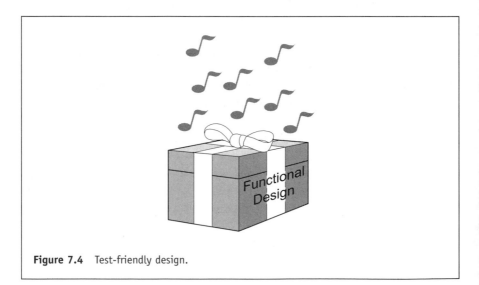

Figure 7.4 Test-friendly design.

these problems over and over again, this has a negative influence on their motivation. Advanced automation has, on the contrary, a positive influence on the testers, because dull and repetitive actions are automated as much as possible.

Checkpoints

[?] The test team is involved in the design and realization to provide optimal testability of the system ('design for test').

[?] The test team has sufficient knowledge and skills to provide a meaningful realization of the checkpoint mentioned above.

[?] The recommendations of the test team are considered 'seriously' by the organization and/or project.

[?] Management supports testers (with people and means) in working continually on the improvement of the test process.

[?] Participation in testing is regarded as a 'promotion'; testing has a high status.

[?] The development process is of sufficient maturity: at least time and quality are controlled.

[?] Test jobs are described at an organization level, including career possibilities and reward structures.

Checkpoints: dependencies

Test strategy, level C, Combined strategy for high-level tests plus low-level tests or evaluation

Moment of involvement, level C, Start of requirements definition

Test tools, level B, Execution and analysis tools

Test engineering implies high maturity of the test process. This means that the test process is involved in the project at an early stage, that the separate test levels are coordinated, and that the test process is sufficiently automated.

Reporting, level C, Risks and recommendations, substantiated with metrics

Meeting the recommendations mentioned in the checkpoints requires a sufficient reporting level.

Improvement suggestions

Propagate the professional test approach in the organization.

Give presentations and training to designers in the field of testing.

Arrange that the functions of tester, test manager, and so on are recognized as separate functions in the personnel department. A comprehensive task description should be drawn up.

Arrange that the testers are (also) appraised on their specific test qualities.

Have the relevant quality requirements formulated in a measurable or, in other words, testable way. Then let the testers assess these requirements for measurability and give appropriate advice ('the system should be easily understandable' cannot be objectively measured).

Bring aspects that increase testability into the functional design and realization, for example built-in visibility and control features. Visibility features are:

- showing status information (internal program variables);

- execution statistics;

- trace information (which path the software took).

Control features are:

- slowing down the execution of a program;

- stopping the execution of a program;

- making the program crash;

- changing the system status (manipulation of the system date!).

These features can be turned on or off.

Also consider the implementation of a built-in test in the software. These tests perform certain standard evaluations, for example whether a data structure is fully filled. This increases trust in the operation of the system and makes problem analysis easier.

Automating the test process has a positive influence on motivation, because dull and repetitive actions do not have to be executed manually.

For advanced automation see the directions in the corresponding level of Test tools.

Train testers and/or employ specific expertise, enabling the test team to make a useful contribution to the development processes mentioned earlier.

Insist that the organization start Software Process Improvement programs to improve the manageability and predictability of the development process.

Carry out Public Relations activities for testing within the organization. This spotlights testing, its advantages, the fact that it is a profession, and so on.

7.12 Test functions and training

In a test process the correct composition of a test team is very important. A mix of the various disciplines, functions, knowledge, and skills is needed. Besides specific test expertise, knowledge of the subject matter to be tested, knowledge of the organization, and general IT knowledge are required. Social skills are also very important. In order to acquire this mix, training, etc. is needed.

7.12.1 Test manager and testers (A)

Description
The contributions of skilled testers are of great importance for a smoothly running test process. A test team wholly consisting of, for example, users or developers has far less chance of realizing a good quality test process.

Besides the specific knowledge and skill that a tester must have, there is also a 'psychological' factor. It has already been indicated (Myers, 1979) that the base attitude of a tester is substantially different from the attitude of a developer: a tester tries to demonstrate the lack of quality of the system and thus actively searches for defects. The developer's attitude is focused more on demonstrating that the system is good.

Checkpoints
- ❓ The test personnel consist at the very least of a test manager and a number of testers.

- ❓ The tasks and responsibilities have been defined.

- ❓ The test personnel has had specific test training (for example, test management, test techniques, etc.) or has sufficient experience in the field of testing.

- ❓ For the acceptance test, expertise in the subject matter is available to the test team.

Checkpoints: dependencies
- None.

Improvement suggestions
Give testers and test managers test training.

Include function descriptions in the test plan, which describe who should perform which task.

Arrange the required subject matter expertise in a timely manner (especially in the case of the acceptance test).

7.12.2 (Formal) Methodical, Technical, and Functional support, Management (B) of test process, testware and infrastructure

Description

Besides employing skilled testers, it is also important to arrange support and management in the test process. Methodical support means giving help in organizing the test process, such as drawing up instructions, helping with defining the test strategy, and so on. Technical support is necessary to organize and operate the infrastructure. Functional support helps to answer functional questions that arise during testing. For these latter two forms of support in particular, parties outside the test process are needed, so it is important to coordinate the effort well and in time. Lack of support can cause much delay in the test process.

Furthermore, attention is focused on the evaluation of the test process: Quality Assurance (QA). This should prevent the process showing all kinds of problems and lapses when it is too late. If you allow these problems to exist it is almost certain that a price must be paid in the form of extra time or money or accepting a lesser test quality.

EXAMPLE 7.11

Inexperienced testers can make many errors in the specification of test cases. When this is discovered in time, corrective actions can easily be taken in the form of extra training and limited rework. Later the damage is much harder to correct.

Checkpoints

[?] The task Methodical Support is outlined separately. Its activities are defining and maintaining test instructions, procedures, and techniques and advising about and evaluating the correct application of the above.

[?] The task Technical Support is outlined separately.

[?] The task Functional Support is outlined separately.

[?] The task Management test process is outlined separately and is responsible for the registration, storage, and availability of all management objects of the test process. Sometimes one will carry out the management oneself, in other cases one will organize and/or evaluate that management. Objects to be managed are progress, budgets, and defects.

[?] The task Management testware is outlined separately and is responsible for the registration, storage, and availability of all management objects of the testware. Sometimes one will carry out the management oneself, in other cases one will organize and/or evaluate that management. Objects to be managed are test documentation, test basis, test objects (internal), test cases including test files and databases, test instructions and procedures.

[?] The task Management test infrastructure is outlined separately and is responsible for the registration, storage, and availability of all management objects of the test infrastructure. Sometimes one will carry out the management oneself, in other cases one will organize and/or evaluate that management. Objects to be managed are test environments (test databases) and test tools.

[?] The persons who carry out these tasks have sufficient knowledge and experience.

[?] The time needed for these tasks is planned. Supervision is carried out to see that these tasks are in fact performed.

Checkpoints: dependencies
[ ] None.

Improvement suggestions
Include function descriptions in the test plan, which describe who should perform which support task.

Allocate capacity for the support tasks and check that this capacity is really used.

Start evaluating the correct use of instructions, procedures, and techniques by giving testers or the test manager simple check activities such as reviewing each other's test specifications, and so on.

7.12.3 Formal internal Quality Assurance (C)

Description
The evaluation of test activities described in the preceding level is expanded further and formalized with a twofold aim:

- Giving confidence in the quality of the test process, which means confidence in the advice provided by testing: this provides more certainty about the quality of the tested object.

- Making continuous improvement of the test process possible.

Checkpoints
[?] Parallel to the test plan, an internal QA plan for testing is formulated.

[?] The person assigned the QA task has no other tasks within the test team.

? The results of QA activities are used as input for further test process improvement.

? The person who performs the QA task has sufficient QA knowledge and experience.

Checkpoints: dependencies

Scope of methodology, level A, Project specific

The QA task means that the test process is evaluated. This task is only useful if the test process at least is supposed to work according to a described process.

Improvement suggestions

Have the role of internal QA performed by a QA or test employee of the line department.

Those to whom the QA person can report are the test manager, the project manager, the test customer, and the line department for testing.

Ensure that the QA results are really used (for example, for further test process improvement) by the test manager, or by the line department for testing.

7.13 Scope of methodology

For each test process in the organization, a certain methodology or working method is employed, with activities, procedures, instructions, techniques, and so on. When these methodologies differ each time or when the methodology is so generic that each time many parts of it have to be worked out again, the efficiency of the test process is decreased. The aim is for the organization to employ a methodology that is sufficiently generic to be applied everywhere, but that contains enough detail so that the wheel does not have to be reinvented each time.

7.13.1 Project specific (A)

Description

Documentation of the working method and the instructions makes clear what the process looks like. This makes the quality of the process less dependent on individuals and shortens the learning time for new people, and the unity of the methodology stimulates manageability and increases process quality. In addition, a documented and structured working method makes improvement possible. When there is no working method, it cannot be improved. Under documentation are items such as methodology, instructions, procedures, techniques, and so on. In the ensuing description the generic term 'methodology' is used.

Checkpoints

☑ A methodology is formulated for each project.

☑ The aspects described cover at least: a description of the full life-cycle model of testing, management of the test process (progress and quality), test product management, and test specification techniques to be used.

☑ The methodology is followed.

Checkpoints: dependencies

▨ Life-cycle model, level A, Planning, Specification, and Execution

▨ Test specification techniques, level B, Formal techniques

▨ Testware management, level A, Internal testware management

▨ Defect management, level A, Internal defect management

Only if the test process meets the levels mentioned above do we speak of a methodology.

▨ Test process management, level B, Planning, execution, monitoring, and adjusting

In addition to describing the methodology, it is important to use it as it is described. To do this, evaluation and adjustment of the process should take place.

Improvement suggestions

Define the methodology in a handbook or test plan or refer to the literature. This will partly consist of putting together existing material.

Assure that there is or will be (as a result of training) sufficient test expertise, to make sure that the methodology described can in fact be followed.

7.13.2 Organization generic (B)

Description

The same advantages as in the preceding level also apply organization-wide. Each new test process does not have to start from scratch, but adopts the existing working method and instructions. Because the approach is similar in multiple projects, the test processes are similar and the testware is more reusable. This facilitates mutual comparison of the test processes, so that the reasons for a test process performing well or less well can be found more quickly. The risk of an organization-wide approach is that either the approach is too generic, causing each test process to have to do a lot of work for itself, or too detailed, giving little breathing space for the specific features of each test process.

Checkpoints

❓ The methodology is defined in a generic model for the organization.

❓ Each project works according to this generic model.

❓ Variances are sufficiently argued and documented.

Checkpoints: dependencies

▨ None.

Improvement suggestions

Define the organization-wide methodology in a handbook or refer to the literature. This will partly consist of putting together existing material. Give much attention to the difference between the generic and the specific: specific issues should not be defined in the organization-wide methodology.

Place the responsibility for formulating and monitoring the methodology with a line department. This department should have enough test expertise to do this.

Arrange structural communication between the projects and this line department (for example, to discuss variances in the instructions).

EXAMPLE 7.12

A distinct form of test organization, which realizes directly that the test methodology does not remain project-specific, is when the test organization is organized as a line department. In this form the test process is regarded as a factory with personnel (testers), machines (infrastructure and tools), and so on. Several customers (projects, etc.) can subcontract their test tasks to this test organization. The customer brings his order to the factory, the order is planned in the form of work orders for the personnel, the machines are adjusted correctly, the order is executed, and the customer can collect the product (the tested object, possible defects, reporting and advice) at the agreed time. The quality norms of the factory guarantee the customer a certain test quality.

Because this process is, generally speaking, the same for each order and because the machines and the personnel are already in the factory, it is much more efficient and can be executed in a much shorter time than would be possible if the factory had to be built from the ground up each time (= for each project). A precondition for such a process is that the order can be handled with the machines available. If a new machine has to be brought in, 'setup time' is needed. Although this approach makes testing faster, cheaper, and better, a number of points of interest are of greater importance than normal:

- good agreements and communication with customers who offer their products for testing (customer, developers, customers);
- having enough working stock;
- having expertise in the subject matter available.

7.13.3 Organization optimizing, R&D activities (C)

Description
A generic approach should not be 'static,' but should be checked and adapted to meet changing circumstances. For developments that are new to the organization (for example, Rapid Application Development), a check should be made to see if the test approach has to be adapted for this. Also, on this level the optimum between generic and detailed is matched as closely as possible.

Checkpoints
? There is a structured feedback process (both formally elicited and actioned by the R&D department) in the generic model.

? Structural maintenance and innovation (R&D) are done on the generic model, for example on the basis of feedback.

Checkpoints: dependencies
Commitment and motivation, level B, Testing integrated in project organization

R&D in the test area requires high commitment from all those involved.

Test process management, level C, Monitoring and adjustment in the organization

A condition for maintenance and innovation on the generic model is that this model is also applied (in the correct manner). This needs monitoring.

Improvement suggestions
Have the line department conduct intake and exit interviews with each test project, in which the organization-wide test model is discussed and evaluated.

Periodically, for example (half) yearly, draw up a plan of issues to be dealt with for maintenance and innovation. Claim resources for the execution of this plan and check the execution.

Take care that the products of maintenance and innovation are included in the generic model and communicate the adaptations to the organization.

7.14 Communication

In a test process, communication will take place in all kinds of ways with the various people involved, within the test team itself as well as with parties such as the developer, user, customer, and so on. These forms of communication are of great importance for a smoothly running test process, both for creating good conditions and coordinating the test strategy as well as for communicating progress and quality.

7.14.1 Internal communication (A)

Description
Good communication between the test team participants is important for a good mutual relationship, motivation, and understanding. This communication also leads to early detection of (arising) problems, so if measures are needed they can be taken in time.

Checkpoints

[?] There is a periodic meeting within the test team. This meeting has a fixed agenda and its main focus is progress (lead time and hours spent) and the quality of the object to be tested.

[?] Periodically, each team member participates in the meeting.

[?] Deviations from the test plan are communicated and documented.

Checkpoints: dependencies
☐ None.

Improvement suggestions
Ask each team member regularly to evaluate the test process, to determine which parts of it are going well and which could be improved.
Provide consistent handling of the actions that arise from the meeting.
Arrange for project news to be announced in the meeting.

7.14.2 Project communication (defects, change control) (B)

Description
Good involvement of the testing in the rest of the project improves mutual relationships and leads to better communication. This often gives more time and possibilities for anticipating coming developments ('Unfortunately, there have been a few slight hiccups; we cannot deliver tomorrow, it will probably take another two months').

Recording agreements increases the controllability of the test process, because it enables a better account, by forcing agreements to be formulated transparently ('I thought you'd said that..., that is the way I understood it'; 'No, I never said that, I said that...').

A structural defects meeting provides smoother handling of defects and the parties understand each other better.

Usually the developer and the customer judge the proposed changes to the test basis or the test object (often called change proposals). Testers can estimate the consequences of the changes for testing. A small change in the specification of the program can cause a large test effort. Thus, involving testers in change control gives more insight into the consequences for time, money, and the quality of the suggested changes, increasing the controllability of the total development process.

Checkpoints

❓ In the test team meeting minutes are taken.

❓ In the test team meeting, besides progress and the quality of the test object, the quality of the test process is a fixed subject on the agenda.

❓ Periodically, the test manager reports progress and the quality of the object to be tested, including the risks, in the project meeting. The test manager also reports the quality of the test process.

❓ Agreements in this meeting are documented.

❓ The test manager is informed in time about changes in planned and agreed delivery dates (test basis as well as test object).

❓ In a periodic defects meeting (or analysis meeting), solutions to defects are discussed between representatives of the test team and of other parties involved.

❓ Testing is involved in change control for judging the impact of change proposals on the test effort.

Checkpoints: dependencies

Reporting, level B, Progress (status of tests and products), activities (costs and time, milestones), defects with priorities

Life-cycle model, level A, Planning, Specification, and Execution

Participation in project meetings in which the test team reports quality and progress means that the test process should be manageable. Use of a life-cycle model is very important here. Also, reporting must be done on a certain level.

▨ Defect management, level A, Internal defect management

A precondition for participating in the defects meeting is that the defects are well managed internally.

Improvement suggestions

Arrange for the (high-level) test to be represented in the project meeting by someone who is not also responsible for other activities (especially development activities). The risk is that otherwise the signals from testing are too muffled.

Make a procedure for the periodic defects meeting. Take into account here the possibility of escalation and of a crash procedure (in case of defects that block the progress of the testing).

Start the defects meeting, paying attention to the learning effect of formulating defects (tester writes: 'calculation incorrect'; developer expects: 'on line 124 in program 23a it says "−" instead of "+"'; this must lead to mutual agreement on good detail in defects). Well-formulated defects reduce sorting out and communication time.

In estimating changes, bear in mind testing for regression. Testing a number of changes together is much cheaper than testing these changes separately (and letting them go to a next phase in the system development). This is, by the way, an important argument for delivering (groups of) changes in releases. Ensure that in estimating changes the above-mentioned issues are taken into account, a precondition being the availability of knowledge about substantiated estimating of tests.

Make it possible for either the test manager or the project manager to give a summarized test report in the steering committee.

7.14.3 Communication within the organization about the quality of the test processes (C)

Description

Improving test processes is a continuous activity. The organization realizes that a well-organized test process contributes much to the manageability of the quality and costs of its information services. Communicating at an organization level ensures that the available knowledge about the test processes arrives at enough people and thus is kept. This makes organizing new test processes (with new people) easier.

Checkpoints

❓ There is a periodic meeting in which propositions for improvement of the test methodology used and the test processes are discussed.

❓ Participants are representatives of the test teams and of the line department for testing.

▨ Scope of methodology, level B, Organization generic

Communication about testing at the organization level is not useful if each test process has a different approach. Therefore, a generic methodology is a precondition.

Improvement suggestions

Appoint someone from the line department (responsible for testing) as a pioneer for the (periodic) meeting.

Draw up a fixed agenda, with points of action, and so on.

Involve the testers of the various test levels in communication (also representatives of the low-level tests).

Involve the developers in communication on an ad-hoc basis.

Check the correct handling of signals and improvement suggestions from the various test processes. It is not a bad thing if a proposition is not accepted, but it is a bad thing if it is never considered again.

Take care, especially at the beginning, that a number of improvement proposals are ready for discussion and that progress about currently running improvements can be reported.

When Software Process Improvement initiatives are also running, it is recommended to involve someone involved in these in communication, keeping both improvement actions in step with each other.

7.15 Reporting

Testing is not so much 'finding defects' as providing insight into the quality level of the product. Therefore reporting is considered the most important product of the test process. Reporting should be focused on giving substantiated advice to the customer concerning the product and even the system development process.

7.15.1 Defects (A)

Description

The first level is that reporting is being done. In this reporting the total number of defects found and those still unsolved is a minimum requirement. This provides a first impression of the quality of the system to be tested. Furthermore, it is important that reporting should take place periodically, because merely reporting at the end gives the project no room for adjustments.

Checkpoints

? The defects found are reported periodically, divided into solved and unsolved defects.

Checkpoints: dependencies

■ None.

Improvement suggestions

Find out approximately how many defects have been found, regardless of whether they have been solved or not.

List the unsolved defects. These are defects that are yet to be solved as well as those that will not be solved, even if the defect is justified (these are the *known errors*).

Arrange for the handling of the defects to be done according to a tight administrative procedure. A condition for this procedure is that it should not cost too much time to draw up the reporting described above.

7.15.2 Progress (status of tests and products), activities (costs and time, milestones), defects with priorities (B)

Description

The test reporting contains extra information in the form of the planned, spent so far, and still required budgets and lead time. This information is relevant because the customer gains faster insight into the costs of testing and the feasibility of the (total) planning. In addition, the reported defects are classified into categories of seriousness. Ten cosmetic defects are probably less serious than one production-blocking defect. This increases insight into the quality of the tested system.

Checkpoints

? The defects are reported, divided into seriousness categories according to clear and objective norms.

? The progress of each test activity is reported periodically and in writing. Aspects reported on are: lead time, hours spent, which tests have been specified, what has been tested, what parts of the object performed correctly and incorrectly and what must still be tested.

Checkpoints: dependencies

▨ Test process management, level B, Planning, execution, monitoring, and adjusting

▨ Life-cycle model, level A, Planning, Specification, and Execution

To report progress, the progress must be known. This means that the test process must be managed.

▨ Defect management, level A, Internal defect management

A precondition for reporting defects is that the defects are well managed internally.

Make the project aware that the mere fact that there are no remaining unsolved defects does not mean that one can conclude that the test gives positive advice. It could be the case, for example, that a defect found in function A has a structural character and is also present in functions B to Z. When the defect is solved for function A, this does not say anything about the possibility that the defect is still present in functions B to Z. The advice could then be to test these functions again, before releasing the test object.

Focus on the most important defects.

By doing progress reporting, what testing does and approximately how much time each activity costs become visible. This increases insight and (mutual) understanding.

7.15.3 Risks and recommendations, substantiated with metrics (C)

Description
Substantiated as much as possible with trend analyses of metrics (budgets, time, and quality (defects)), risks are indicated with regard to (parts of) the tested object. Risks can be, for example, not meeting the date on which the object has to be taken into production or the tested object being of insufficient quality. For the risks recommendations are made which focus mainly on the activities of testing. Such advice can be, for example, to execute a full retest for subsystem A and a limited retest for subsystem B. The main advantage is that such reporting makes it possible for the customer to take measures in time. Substantiating the advice with trend analyses provides the customer with the arguments for taking the (often costly) measures.

Checkpoints
- [?] A quality judgment on the test object is made. The judgment is based on the acceptance criteria, if present, and related to the test strategy.

- [?] Possible trends with respect to progress and quality are reported periodically and in writing.

- [?] The reporting contains risks (for the customer) and recommendations.

- [?] The quality judgment and the detected trends are substantiated with metrics (from defect administration and progress monitoring).

Checkpoints: dependencies
- Metrics, level A, Project metrics (product)

- Defect management, level B, Extensive defect management with flexible reporting facilities.

Substantiation with metrics for reporting minimally requires these levels:

▪ Test strategy, level A, Strategy for single high-level test

▪ Test specification techniques, level B, Formal techniques

To make a substantiated judgment on the system to be tested, insight into the risks is required. Also, the test strategy should be based on these risks.

Improvement suggestions

Take the chosen test strategy as a starting point. Did we deviate from it? Was this strategy already 'thin'? Did retesting still proceed in a structured manner? How large is the chance of regression? Ask these questions for each quality characteristic to be tested. Try to estimate the risks on the basis of the answers and propose measures.

Substantiate the most important conclusions with facts if possible: metrics from progress monitoring and defect administration.

EXAMPLE 7.13

An example of the contents of a progress report:

1 Introduction

2 Agreements

3 Performed activities
   3.1 Progress overview
   3.2 Trends, remarks, and recommendations about progress

4 Quality
   4.1 Quality indicators
   4.2 Trends, remarks, and recommendations about quality

5 Bottlenecks and discussion items

6 Activities in the coming period

The contents of an end report are more or less the same as for a progress report:

1 (Management conclusion)

2 Introduction

3 Agreements

4 Evaluation test object
   4.1 General
   4.2 Release advice

7.15.4 Recommendations have a Software Process Improvement character (D)

Description

In this form of reporting the recommendations deal not merely with test activities, but also with activities outside testing, that is, the entire system development process. For example, recommendations to perform (extra) reviews of the functional specifications, to organize version management, or to take into account in the project planning the required time for transferring software. In this form of reporting, testing focuses somewhat more on improving the process rather than the product and more on the prevention of defects (or in any case detecting them as soon as possible).

Checkpoints

❓ Advice is given not only on the area of testing but also on other parts of the project.

Checkpoints: dependencies

▨ Test strategy, level C, Combined strategy for tests plus low-level tests or evaluation

To advise other project parts, it is important that all test processes form a consistent whole and are well coordinated. The advice is only valuable if it is given with sufficient insight into the total test process (the advice should 'exceed testing').

▨ Commitment and motivation, level C, Test engineering

Furthermore, the organization should have a high level of commitment for the test process to take test advice for other project parts 'seriously.'

Improvement suggestions

Start small, with recommendations that are valid only for the project.

Involve the line departments in a later phase, because Software Process Improvement goes beyond projects (and the maintenance organization, etc.).

Let the line departments coordinate and monitor the recommendations.

7.16 Defect management

Although the administration of defects is in fact a project matter and not specifically confined to the testers, they are the people most involved. Good administration should be able to monitor the life cycle of a defect and also give various (statistical) overviews. These overviews are, for instance, used to make substantiated quality statements.

7.16.1 Internal defect management (A)

Description
Recording defects in an administration helps to provide good administrative handling and monitoring, and is also a source of information about the quality of the system. The importance of handling and monitoring is that defects must not remain unsolved without a decision having been made by the right person. This means, for example, that a developer can never dismiss a defect as unjust without another person having looked at it.

To get an impression of the quality of a system, it is interesting to know not only that there are no outstanding open defects, but also the total number of defects and their type.

Checkpoints
? The different stages of the life cycle of defects are administrated (up to and including retest).

? The following items are recorded about the defect:
- unique number
- person entering the defect
- date
- seriousness category
- problem description
- status indication

Checkpoints: dependencies
None.

Improvement suggestions
Maintaining such an administration can be done with a spreadsheet or word processor, unless:

- a very large number of defects are expected (for example, in a large project), and/or
- comprehensive reporting possibilities are required (see also the next level).

For those cases it is better to use a specific tool for defect administration.

Define the task Intermediary in the test team or in the project. The aim of this task is to channel the defects and their solutions adequately. The intermediary has external contacts about this on an executive level. The intermediary functions as a middleman of defects on the one hand and solutions on the other. The advantages are that the quality of the defects and solutions is more carefully checked and that communication is streamlined.

A basic procedure for defects is shown in Figure 7.5.

The analysis meeting is a work-floor meeting in which representatives of testers, subject matter experts, and developers participate, among others. In

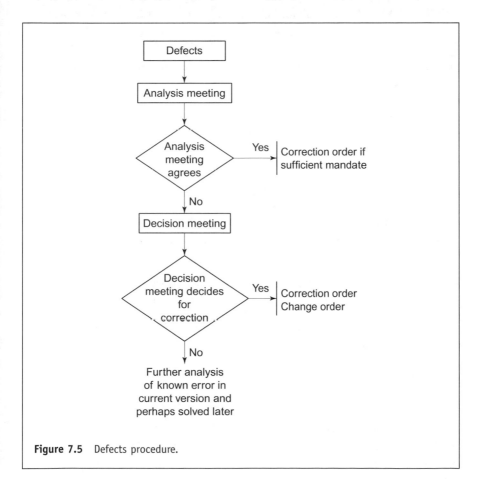

Figure 7.5 Defects procedure.

this meeting the handling of defects is decided. If no agreement can be reached or if a defect has too large an impact, it is passed over to a decision meeting. The project leader and possibly even the customer are present in this meeting.

7.16.2 Extensive defect management with flexible reporting facilities (B)

Description

Data relevant to good handling is recorded for the various defects. This clarifies, for solving as well as for retesting, which part of the test basis or the test object the defect relates to and which test case detected the defect. By using comprehensive reporting, aggregated information can be gathered, which helps in spotting trends as soon as possible. Trends are, for example, an observation that most of the defects relate to (a part of) the functional specifications, or that the defects are mainly concentrated on the screen handling. This information can be used in its turn to take timely measures.

Checkpoints

? Defect data needed for later trend analyses is recorded in detail:
- test case
- test
- subsystem
- priority (test blocking Y/N)
- program + version
- test basis + version
- cause (probable + definitive)
- all status transitions of the defect including dates
- a description of the problem solution
- (version of) test object in which the defect is solved
- problem solver.

? The administration lends itself to extensive reporting possibilities, which means that reports can be selected and sorted in different ways.

? There is someone responsible for ensuring that defect administration is carried out properly and consistently.

Checkpoints: dependencies

None.

Improvement suggestions

Such defect administration usually requires automated support (self-built or a commercial package).

Indicate the importance of prioritizing the defects: to make discussions easier, make procedures run faster, and gain more insight into the test results. A special point of interest is arranging for quick handling of defects that block test progress.

7.16.3 Project defect management (C)

Description
Using one single defect administration for the entire project is a great advantage. All parties involved in system development – developers, users, testers, QA people, etc. – can put defects as well as solutions for defects into it. This greatly simplifies communication concerning the handling of defects. Also, a central administration provides extra possibilities for retrieving information. A point of interest is authorizations, which means that unwanted changing or closing of defects must not be possible.

Checkpoints

? The defect administration is used integrally in the project. The defects originate from the various disciplines, those who perform the solution add their solution to the administration themselves, and so on.

? Authorizations ensure that each user of the administration can do only what he or she is allowed to do.

Checkpoints: dependencies

None.

Improvement suggestions
Defining authorizations well – or having a good understanding of how to use the defect management system – are of importance here, because otherwise there is insufficient certainty that defects can be looked after properly.

Defect administration that is too limited, however, cannot be used throughout the project. When the defect administration largely meets level B (that is, not quite!) it can be useful to use the defect administration in the entire project.

7.17 Testware management

The products of testing should be maintainable and reusable and must therefore be managed. As well as the products of the testing itself, such as test plans, test specifications, and test databases, it is also important that the products of preceding processes such as design and realization are managed well, because the test process can be greatly disturbed by the delivery of wrong software versions, and so on. By making demands on the management as a tester, a positive influence is exerted and the testability of the test objects is increased.

7.17.1 Internal testware management (A)

Description

Good (version) management of the internal testware, such as test specifications, test files, and test databases, is required for the fast execution of (re-)tests. This ensures not too much time is lost just before test execution should start in finding out what has to be tested and what items are related. Also, changes in the test basis will cause revision of test cases. To find out which test cases are involved, the relationship between the test basis and test cases is very important.

Checkpoints

[?] The testware (test cases, starting test databases, etc.), test basis, test object, test documentation, and test guidelines are managed internally according to a described procedure, containing steps for delivery, registration, archiving, and referring.

[?] The management comprises the relationships between the various parts (test basis, test object, testware, etc.).

[?] Transfer to the test team takes place according to a standard procedure. The parts comprising a transfer should be known: which parts and versions of the test object, which (version of the) test basis, solved defects, and still unsolved defects, including those from the developer himself.

Checkpoints: dependencies

[ ] None.

Improvement suggestions

Make someone responsible for testware management, but preferably not the test manager, because he or she is the 'customer.'

Define the management procedure and communicate this procedure. An example of the basic steps is given below.

EXAMPLE 7.14

The four steps from the procedure Testware management:

Delivery

- The products to be managed are delivered by the testers to the testware manager. The products must be delivered complete (with date and version stamp). The manager does a completeness check. Products in an electronic form should follow a standard naming convention, which also specifies the version number.

Registration

- The testware manager registers the delivered products in his or her administration with reference to, among other things, the supplier's name, product name, date, and version number.

    In registering changed products, the manager should check that consistency between the different products remains guaranteed.

Archiving

- A distinction is made between new and changed products. In general it can be said that new products are added to the archive and changed products replace the preceding version.

Reference

- Issuing products to project team members or third parties takes place by means of a copy of the requested products. The manager registers which version of the products is issued to whom and when.

Supply memory aids in the form of, for example, questions or entry sections in testware templates.

Look into the possibility of using version management tools.

7.17.2 External management of test basis and test object (B)

Description

Good management of the test basis and the test object is a project responsibility. When the management of the test basis and the test object is well organized, testing can make a simple statement about the quality of the system. A great risk in insufficient management is, for example, that the version of the software that eventually goes into production differs from the tested version.

Checkpoints

- ☐ The test basis and the test object (usually design and software) are managed by the project according to a described procedure, with steps for delivery, registering, archiving, and reference.

- ☐ Management contains the relationships between the various parts (test basis and test object).

■ The test team is informed about changes in the test basis or test object in a timely fashion.

Checkpoints: dependencies

■ None.

Improvement suggestions

Try to collect a number of examples of what went wrong as a result of wrong (external) version management. Use these to make the project and the management aware of the importance of version management, from a testing point of view as well as from a project point of view.

When version management is insufficiently rigorous, indicate the associated risks in the test advice: 'The system we have tested is of good quality, but we have no certainty that this will be the production version or that this is the version that the customer expects to get.' Also indicate how much the test process has suffered from insufficient version management, for example that much analysis has been necessary and/or many unnecessary defects have been found.

Ensure good communication with the project and the developer.

Gain insight into the way in which external management is/should be coordinated ('narrow-mindedness' is often the cause of bad version management; each department or group has its own version management or has the relevant components well organized, but coherence between the various components is insufficiently managed).

If necessary, investigate the process for version management of the project and give recommendations.

7.17.3 Reusable testware (C)

Description

Making the testware reusable prevents the labor-intensive specification of test cases in the next project phase or maintenance phase having to be done again. Although this may sound completely logical, practice shows that in the stressed period immediately before the release-to-production date, keeping testware properly up to date is often not feasible, and after completion of the test it never happens. It is, however, almost impossible to reuse another person's incomplete, not yet actualized testware. Because the maintenance organization usually reuses only a limited part of the testware, it is important to transfer that part carefully. Making good agreements, such as arranging beforehand which testware has to be transferred fully and properly up to date, is an enormous help in preventing test cases having to be specified again.

Checkpoints

? (A selection, which is agreed beforehand, of) the test products are completed after the end of the test (= fully and up to date) and transferred to the maintenance organization, after which the transfer is formally agreed.

? The transferred test products are actually reused.

Checkpoints: dependencies

░ Test specification techniques, level B, Formal techniques

To make the testware portable, the working method (how the testware is realized) should be clear to everyone. This means that techniques have to be employed.

Improvement suggestions

Provide good communication with the maintenance organization (or the next project).

The maintenance organization must in fact do the testing with the transferred testware. Is it possible to lend testers from the current test team to the maintenance organization for a short time, to simplify and secure the reuse of the testware? Also, the maintenance organization must have or acquire knowledge of the test techniques used.

The problem in actualizing testware lies particularly in the fact that relatively small changes in the test basis can have large consequences for the testware. When the functional specification is revised in 10 minutes and the programmer implements the change in 2 hours, is it acceptable for the actual testing of the change to take 4 hours, plus the 20 hours needed to adapt the testware? A possible solution to this dilemma is reducing the amount of testware that needs to be complete and up to date at all times. This restriction is dependent on the following expectations:

• How many times is the testware to be (re-)used?

• How much time does it take to do an actualization each time, compared to the time needed to totally specify the test cases all over again?

It is therefore of great importance to make solid agreements about this.

EXAMPLE 7.15

In a very large test project for a government department, it turns out that after finishing a release of the new system, frequently only the testware that is used to test a change is adapted. Several parts of the testware have not been adapted to the constant flow of functional changes.

A total update is estimated to be a 1200-hour effort. It is expected that only a part of the testware will be reused. However, it cannot be determined which part of the testware this is, making it inevitable that all testware must be kept up to date. As a (compromise) solution the choice is made to bring only the logical level of the test cases up to date, an activity which is estimated at 400 hours. When a certain part of the testware is being reused, only the lowest and most detailed level of the test cases is adapted or re-specified. This is seen as a good compromise between a total update and performing a full specification of the test cases each time in the future.

7.17.4 Traceability system requirements to test cases (D)

Description

The products of the different phases of the development cycle are mutually related: the system requirements are translated into a functional design, which in turn is translated into a technical design, on the basis of which the programs are coded. Test cases are made from the test basis (the system requirements and/or the functional and/or technical design) and executed on the test object (software, user's manual, etc.). Good management of these relationships presents a number of advantages for testing:

- There is much insight into the quality and depth of the test because for all system requirements, the functional and technical design, and the software, it is known which test cases have been used to check them (or will be). This reduces the chance of omissions in the test.

- When there are changes in the test basis or test object, the test cases to be adapted and/or re-executed can be traced quickly.

- When, as a result of severe time pressure, it is not possible to execute all planned tests, test cases will have to be canceled. Because the relationship with requirements, specifications, and programs is known, it is possible to cancel those test cases whose related requirement or specification causes the smallest risk for operation and it is clear for which requirements or specifications less substantiated statements about the quality are made.

Checkpoints

? Each system requirement and specification is related to one or more test cases in a transparent way, and vice versa.

? These relations are traceable through separate versions (for example, system requirement A, version 1.0, is related to functional design B, version 1.3, is related to programs C and D, versions 2.5 and 2.7, and is related to test cases X to Z, version 1.4).

░ None.

Improvement suggestions
Do not involve only the specifications in the test basis, but also include the system requirements. Often this will mean some researching has to be done.

The non-functional quality requirements are often not clearly formulated. Start a discussion about how these are to be measured and judged.

This level refers to the project or the organization more than to the test process itself. Keep this in mind.

In testware management, provide good links between the test cases, the test basis, and the test object. This requires good version management.

7.18 Test process management

The four steps from the Deming circle (Deming, 1992) are essential for managing each process and each activity (Figure 7.6): each activity is planned, executed, checked, and if necessary acted upon; in other words: 'Say what you do, do what you say.'

A controlled test process is of the utmost importance for executing a test as well as possible in an often turbulent test process.

The starting level is characterized by a lack of planning; the execution of activities starts directly.

7.18.1 Planning and execution (A)

Description
An important step is that with respect to the activities to be executed, the what, how, and when are considered in advance: a planning of the activities takes place. The advantages of this are that it becomes clear more quickly what must be done, when it must be done, and how much resources and

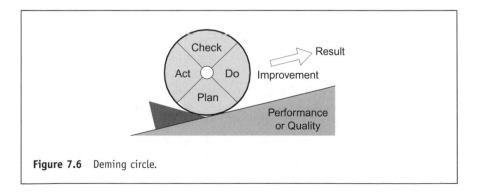

Figure 7.6 Deming circle.

time are required. This can be taken into account in the total project planning. This level bears a great resemblance to level A of the key area Life-cycle model.

Checkpoints

? Prior to the actual test activities, a test plan is formulated in which all activities to be performed are mentioned. For each activity there is an indication of the period in which it runs, the resources (people or means) required, and the products to be delivered.

Checkpoints: dependencies

None.

Improvement suggestions

See key area Life-cycle model, level A.

It is useful to cluster smaller activities into a single activity.

7.18.2 Planning, execution, monitoring, and adjusting (B)

Description

When activities are planned, in itself this is no guarantee of (correct) execution. Each test process is characterized by a certain amount of chaos. As a result, it is the rule rather than the exception that in the course of the process new activities are started, other activities suddenly turn out to be irrelevant, or activities are performed in a different way from that prescribed. The monitoring of the (execution of the) activities is of great importance in ensuring that at completion everything that should have been executed has been executed (not too much, but not too little). Besides monitoring, adjustment is also needed, either by adapting the plans, or by adapting that which must be performed or will be performed.

Checkpoints

? Monitoring of the execution of all planned activities takes place.

? Each activity is also monitored in terms of time and money.

? Deviations are documented.

? In the case of deviations, adjustments are made, either by adjusting the plan, or by performing activities again according to the plan. The adjustment is substantiated.

Checkpoints: dependencies

None.

Improvement suggestions
Deviations and the possible adjustments can be recorded in a new version of the test plan, but can also be defined in the project minutes.

Have the customer of the test agree the deviations and adjustments.

Arrange that at the end it is easy to produce an overview of these deviations.

7.18.3 Monitoring and adjustment within the organization (C)

Description
Monitoring and adjustment of the different test processes also take place at the organizational level, albeit on a much more general level. Here the main concerns are the monitoring and adjustment of the quality of the test processes, such as applying the prescribed methodology (methods, standards, techniques, and procedures).

Checkpoints

[?] At an organizational level, there is monitoring of the application of the methodology (methods, standards, techniques, and procedures) of the organization.

[?] Deviations are documented and reported to the test process.

[?] In the case of deviations the risks are analyzed and adjustments are made, for example by adapting the methodology or by adapting activities or products so that they still meet the methodology. The adjustment is substantiated.

Checkpoints: dependencies

▨ Scope of methodology, level B, Organization generic

Monitoring and adjustment at the organization level is only possible if all test processes in the organization apply a similar working method.

Improvement suggestions
Make (someone in) the line department responsible for monitoring the application of the methodology.

Provide checklists, etc., on the basis of which the evaluation takes place.

7.19 Evaluation

The term evaluation refers to the inspection of intermediate products such as the functional design. The major importance of evaluation is that defects can be found much sooner in the development process than with testing. This makes the rework costs much lower. Also, evaluation can be easily organized, because there are no programs to run, no environment to organize, and so on.

7.19.1 Evaluation techniques (A)

Description

Evaluations, reviews, and so on prove again and again to be the most efficient and effective way to find defects in (the intermediate products of) a system. In practice, good intentions tend to get bogged down by practical execution problems: 'Can you have look at these six folders containing functional specifications? Please return them the day after tomorrow, because then the building starts.' Techniques, in the form of process descriptions and checklists, help to make this manageable. Having multiple techniques available is important because, like testing, not all intermediate products have to be inspected equally thoroughly.

Checkpoints

☑ In evaluating (intermediate) products techniques are used; in other words, a formal and described working method is applied.

☑ The evaluation and its results are reported.

☑ The handling of the results is monitored.

☑ Testers are involved in these evaluations.

Checkpoints: dependencies

☐ None.

Improvement suggestions

Make various evaluation techniques available from which a choice can be made in determining an evaluation strategy. Examples of evaluation techniques are: Fagan inspections, walkthroughs, and buddy checks. Each technique consists in general of the following phases:

- **Plan** In this phase the risk areas are identified and it is decided which analysis methods can best be applied (that is, how can we prevent only spelling or style errors being detected?). The results are recorded in a review plan, together with who, what, when, and the required effort.

- **Assessment** An assessment can take different forms: information and/or research and/or discussion. The organizer draws up an agenda, the products to be researched are inspected, and the defects found are logged. Larger defects are administrated and checked; in case of smaller defects this is often done by the author.

- **Rework** The defects are corrected. For certain larger defects, there can be negotiation as to whether they should be solved, and certain smaller defects can be postponed.

  The differences from the previous versions are documented.

- **Check** Check that all changes take place and a summary report is made.

  Most evaluation techniques are based on the above-mentioned generic life-cycle model, variations being mainly in the form of assessment applied:

  Buddy check: Plan, (Information), Research, Rework, Check
  Walkthrough: Plan, Information, Rework, Check
  etc.

Provide each evaluation technique used with such a (mini) life-cycle model, in which is described what should be done when and who should do it.

A problem with formal evaluations is that re-evaluations are often regarded as too expensive. It is necessary to prevent evaluation of rework activities not being done at all because of this. It is better to have the re-evaluation carried out in a simplified manner.

Ensure that the defects reported from the evaluations are managed. The solution of important defects should be checked.

7.19.2 Evaluation strategy (B)

Description
Just like a test strategy, an evaluation strategy is of vital importance in optimizing the use of resources and as a means of communication with the customer.

By using strategy determination, it is possible to analyze what, where, and how many evaluations must be made to find the optimal balance between the desired (insight into) quality and the required amount of time/money. An optimization takes place with the aim of distributing the available resources correctly among the activities to be performed.

Checkpoints
? A conscious consideration of the product risks takes place.

? There is a differentiation in the area of consideration and the depth of the evaluations, depending on the risks taken and, if present, the acceptance criteria: not all (parts of) intermediate products are evaluated equally; this also goes for quality characteristics.

? Choices are made from multiple evaluation techniques, suitable for the desired depth of an evaluation.

▢ For re-evaluation a (simple) strategy determination takes place, in which a conscious choice of variations between 'evaluate solutions only' and 'complete re-evaluation' is made.

▢ The strategy is determined and subsequently executed. It is checked that the execution of the evaluations takes place according to the strategy; if necessary, adjustments are made.

Checkpoints: dependencies

▨ None.

Improvement suggestions

Indicate the risks in the current working method, or indicate that evaluations can be done more cheaply or quickly.

If there is only one technique available, try to put more or less depth into it by means of simple variations. An example of more or less depth might be involving or not involving certain persons, or limiting or increasing the number of questions.

For re-evaluations, draw up a working method in which a conscious consideration must be made (and documented) each time between a complete re-evaluation and a 'thin' re-evaluation (for each defect, subsystem, or intermediate product).

Discuss the different intermediate products and quality characteristics with the customer and try to find out their relative importance.

Eventually, execute a full strategy determination. The steps that have to be taken to arrive at an evaluation strategy are described in the following paragraphs.

- **Determine quality characteristics** In communication with the customer and possibly other people involved, determine the quality characteristics on which the evaluations are to focus. During the evaluation process, reports on the selected quality characteristics must be given to the customer.

- **Determine relative importance of quality characteristics** Based on the results from the preceding step, indicate how the evaluation effort should be distributed among the selected quality characteristics. The basic principle is that the evaluation of each quality characteristic is equally time-consuming.

- **Subdivide intermediate products or subsystems** This steps divides the IT system into intermediate products and, if necessary, into further subsystems. The division is in principle the same as made in the design documentation. If there is deviation from this division, it must be clearly motivated and described.

- **Determine relative importance of intermediate products or subsystems** Based on the results from the preceding step, indicate how the evaluation effort should be distributed among the recognized intermediate products or subsystems. The basic principle here is that the evaluation of each product is equally time-consuming. Next, indicate for each intermediate product or subsystem which quality characteristics are applicable and how thoroughly these should be evaluated, in relation to the assigned interests.

- **Determine evaluation techniques to be used** As a final step in the evaluation strategy, select evaluation techniques for evaluating the selected quality characteristics and the recognized subsystems.

7.20 Low-level testing

The low-level tests are performed by developers. Well-known low-level tests are the unit test and the integration test. Like evaluation, these tests can find defects at an earlier stage of the system development path than high-level tests do. Low-level tests are efficient, because they require little communication and often the finder is also both the person who caused the defect and the person who corrects it.

However, the quality of the executed tests is often lower. This is because a developer has a different basic attitude from a tester: a developer wants to demonstrate that the system works correctly; a tester tries to discover the difference between the required and the delivered quality (by a specific search for defects).

7.20.1 Low-level test life-cycle model (planning, specification, and execution) (A)

Description
The major advantage of low-level tests following a more structured working method is that the process can be managed better and insight into the quality of these tests increases. If certain information regarding the test activities is not recorded (for example, when the activities start, who executes the test, and what the test consists of), the test process is not manageable. Furthermore, no insight into the quality of the tested object can be obtained and other test levels must deliver more effort to provide a certain level of insight into the quality.

Checkpoints
[?] For the low-level test (at least) the following phases are recognized: planning, specification, and execution. These are performed in sequence, for each subsystem, if applicable.

Activities to be performed for each phase are mentioned below. Each activity is supplied with sub-activities and/or aspects. These are meant as additional information and are not obligatory.

- For the Planning phase:

Activity	Sub-activities/aspects	Product
Formulate assignment	Customer and supplier Area of consideration Aim Preconditions Starting points	Determined in test plan or building plan
Determine test basis	Determine relevant documentation Identify documentation	Determined in test plan or building plan
Set up organization	Determine required functions Allocate tasks, authorizations, and responsibilities Describe organization Allocate personnel	Determined in test plan or building plan
Set up test products	Determine test products Formulate norms and standards	Determined in test plan or building plan
Define infrastructure and tools	Define test environment Define test tools	Determined in test plan or building plan
Set up management	Define test process management (progress, quality, reporting) Define test product management Define defect procedure	Determined in test plan or building plan
Determine planning	Formulate global planning	Determined in test plan or building plan
Produce and agree test plan	Determine risks, threats and measures Determine test plan Agree test plan (customer approval)	Test plan or building plan

- For the Specification phase:

Activity	Sub-activities/aspects	Product
Design test cases and test scripts	Test cases Define starting test databases Test scripts	Test cases Definition of starting test databases Test scripts

- For the Execution phase:

Activity	Sub-activities/aspects	Product
Set up starting test databases		Starting test databases
Execute (re-)tests	Execute test scripts Execute static tests (incl. Evaluation of test results and analysis of differences)	Test defects Test reports

Checkpoints: dependencies

None.

Improvement suggestions

Starting in time with low-level test preparations should become the normal working method as soon as possible.

Developers and testers but also the project management should be made aware that the return on the investment in the planning and preparation of testing is a shorter lead time for test execution and a higher quality of the performed tests. Because test execution is usually on the critical path, the lead time of the total project also becomes shorter. Also, the parties mentioned must be made aware that a good quality low-level test leads to overall lower rework costs (Boehm, 1979).

Employ test expertise to get the low-level tests going.

Make sure that there is some independence between the low-level tester and the programmer (for example, by specification of the test cases of function X by someone other than the programmer).

'The Specialist Interest Group In Software Testing (SIGIST) of the British Computer Society (BCS) has passed the "Standard for Software Component Testing" to the British Standards Institution (BSI) with the aim of them becoming National (and then International) Standards. BS 7925-2, Software component testing, addresses the area of unit testing. The standard describes a generic testing process to give a consistent frame of reference within the standard. It defines a variety of testing techniques to choose from, including black box and white box techniques. Both test case design and related test measurement techniques are described. An annexe contains guidelines for applying the techniques, with each explained by examples.'

(excerpt from a BCS SIGIST Web publication)

7.20.2 White-box techniques (B)

Description
The use of techniques in the developers' tests leads to an increase in the quality of these tests and, as a result, in the quality of the software. The importance of this is that as many defects as possible are detected as early as possible. In addition, the structured working method leads to (a) preventing defects, because the developer has more insight into where defects occur, and to (b) possibilities for process improvement, because in case of a described and structured working method it is clearer where and how improvements can be made.

Much attention will have to be given to getting the developers to use the techniques, because their first reaction to testing is that it is largely superfluous, not creative, and boring ('I'm a good programmer, always ready on time. I make few mistakes. Now, do I have to spend a lot of time demonstrating that my program works OK? While we have a test team who do it much more thoroughly and even like it? Nonsense!').

Checkpoints
- [?] Besides informal techniques, low-level tests use also formal techniques, providing an unambiguous route from the test basis to test cases.

- [?] For low-level tests it is possible to make a substantiated statement about the level of coverage of the test set (compared to the test basis).

- [?] The testware is reusable (within the test team) by a uniform working method.

Implementation of these checkpoints does not mean that AOH (any old how) techniques are not allowed anymore. There is still a place for these techniques. However, in addition to the AOH techniques more formal techniques must be used, which are portable and well documented. This enables a statement to be made about the level of coverage: certain parts of the system are tested thoroughly with a formal technique; other (less important) parts are indeed tested but insight into the quality and depth of the executed test is lacking.

■ None.

Improvement suggestions
See the directions for key area Test specification techniques, level B.

Start with informal techniques, for example by giving each condition to be tested on a copy of the test basis a check mark when the condition has been tested.

Communicate the importance and the advantages of white-box test techniques to the people involved.

Gain an insight into the quality and depth of low-level tests by using light test specification techniques. The use of heavy and formal techniques will be accepted less easily.

7.20.3 Low-level test strategy (C)

Description
The customer of a test expects certain qualities of the system to be delivered which are very different for each system. It is of vital importance to be able to communicate with the customer about this, and depending on the wishes of the customer, to translate this to the way in which testing takes place.

A risk assessment forms the basis of the test strategy, because it is important to optimize the test effort (read: test coverage). By means of strategy determination it is possible to analyze what, where, and how much should be tested to find the optimal balance between the desired quality and the amount of time/money required. Optimization takes place with the aim of distributing the available resources among the test activities to be performed.

Checkpoints
? A motivated consideration of the product risks takes place, for which knowledge of the system, its use, and its operational management is required.

? There is a differentiation with respect to the area of consideration and the depth of the tests, depending on the risks taken and, if present, the acceptance criteria: not all kinds of programs are tested equally thoroughly; this is also the case for quality characteristics.

? One or multiple formal or informal test specification techniques are used, suitable for the desired test depth.

? For retests a (simple) strategy determination also takes place, in which a substantiated choice is made between variations of 'test solutions only' and 'complete retest.'

Table 7.1 Overview of dependencies

	Key area	Level A	Level B	Level C	Level D
1	Test strategy	Strategy for single high-level test (5a, 11a)	Combined strategy for high-level tests (2a, 5b, 11b, 14b, 18b)	Combined strategy for high-level tests plus either low-level tests or evaluation ((20c) or (3c, 19b))	Combined strategy for all test and evaluation levels (3c, 19, 20c)
2	Life-cycle model	Planning, Specification, Execution (11a)	Planning, Preparation, Specification, Execution, and Completion (6a, 17a)		
3	Moment of involvement	Completion of test basis (2a)	Start of test basis (2b)	Start of requirements definition	Project initiation (11c)
4	Estimating and planning	Substantiated estimating and planning (2a)	Statistically substantiated estimating and planning (7b, 15b)		
5	Test specification techniques	Informal techniques	Formal techniques (12a, 17a)		
6	Static test techniques	Inspection of test basis	Checklists		
7	Metrics	Project metrics (product) (11b, 15b, 16a, 18b)	Project metrics (process) (15c, 16b)	System metrics (13b, 14c, 18c)	Organization metrics (>1 system)
8	Test tools	Planning and control tools	Execution and analysis tools (5b, 12a)	Extensive automation of the test process	
9	Test environment	Managed and controlled test environment (12a)	Testing in the most suitable environment (1b)	'Environment-on-call'	
10	Office environment	Adequate and timely office environment			

#		A	B	C	D
11	Commitment and motivation	Assignment of budget and time	Testing integrated in project organization (2a, 15b, 16a, 18b)	Test-engineering (1c, 3c, 8b, 15c)	
12	Test functions and training	Test manager and testers	(Formal) Methodical, Technical, and Functional Support, Management	Formal internal Quality Assurance (13a)	
13	Scope of methodology	Project specific (2a, 5b, 16a, 17a, 18b)	Organization generic	Organization optimizing, R&D activities (11b, 18c)	
14	Communication	Internal communication	Project communication (defects, change control) (2a, 15b, 16a)	Communication in organization about the quality of the test processes (13b)	
15	Reporting	Defects	Progress (status of tests and products), activities (costs and time, milestones), defects with priorities (2a, 16a, 18b)	Risks and recommendations, substantiated with metrics (1a, 5b, 7a, 16b)	Recommendations have a Software Process Improvement character (1c, 11c)
16	Defect management	Internal defect management	Extensive defect management with flexible reporting facilities	Project defect management	
17	Testware management	Internal testware management	External management of test basis and test object	Reusable testware (5b)	Traceability system requirements to test cases
18	Test process management	Planning and execution	Planning, execution, monitoring, and adjusting	Monitoring and adjusting within organization (13b)	
19	Evaluation	Evaluation techniques	Evaluation strategy		
20	Low-level testing	Low-level test life-cycle model (planning, specification, and execution)	White-box techniques	Low-level test strategy	

? The strategy is determined and subsequently executed. It is checked that the execution of the tests takes place according to the strategy. If necessary, adjustments are made.

Checkpoints: dependencies
None.

Improvement suggestions
See the instructions for key area Test strategy, level A.

Without question it is a good thing that developers test their own work. Do realize, however, the pros and cons of it. The advantage is that the developer knows his or her own work well and can therefore formulate and execute appropriate test cases quickly. In addition, if problems are found the developer can quickly trace the cause and solve the problem. The disadvantage is that the developer will not discover his or her own 'blind spots.' Consider therefore the possibility of developers testing each other's work (for example, randomly or in integration tests).

7.21 Overview of dependencies

For each level in Table 7.1 the dependencies on other levels are given in parentheses. For example, in key area Test strategy, level A, two dependencies are mentioned: 5a and 11a. The number indicates the key area and the letter the level, so this level is dependent on Test specification techniques, level A, and Commitment and motivation, level A.

TPI available on the Internet

At the Internet address http://www.iquip.nl/tpi, a spreadsheet (in Microsoft Excel format) is available containing an overview of all checkpoints for each level, grouped by key area. This spreadsheet (Table A.1) can be used as a basis for composing your own inquiry forms.

Table A.1 The layout of the spreadsheet.

No.	**Key area**/*Level*/Checkpoint	*OK?*	*Comments*
1	**Test strategy**		
1.A	*Strategy for single high-level test (A)*		
1.A.1	A motivated consideration of product risks takes place, requiring knowledge of the system, and the use and management of the system.		
1.A.2	There is a differentiation in the depth of the tests, depending on the risks taken and, if available, the acceptance criteria: not all subsystems are tested equally thoroughly; this also applies to each quality characteristic.		
etc.	etc.		

Various other TPI products are also available at this address. It is also possible to ask questions, to make remarks and to arrange to be kept informed about TPI innovations and practical results. The website is in English, German and Dutch.

Summary of TMap

Despite encouraging results with various quality improvement approaches, the IT industry is still far from achieving zero defect software. Testing will remain an important activity within software development and maintenance, often taking more than 30–40% of the total budget. Both the increasing importance of software in society and the costs involved in testing confirm the need to structure the testing process. This appendix provides an outline description of TMap, the **Test Management approach** for structured testing (for both low-level and high-level tests) of software products. (TMap is a registered trademark of IQUIP Informatica B.V., The Netherlands.) It provides answers to the what, when, how, where, and who questions of testing. To structure the organization and execute the test processes, TMap is based on four cornerstones (Figure B.1):

- a development process-related life-cycle model for the testing activities (L);
- solid organizational embedding (O);

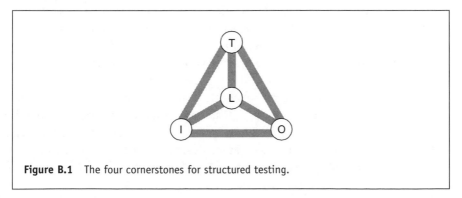

Figure B.1 The four cornerstones for structured testing.

- the right resources and infrastructure (I);

- usable techniques for the various testing activities (T).

In recent years TMap has evolved toward the standard for software testing in The Netherlands. It is being used by more than two hundred Dutch organizations. Most Dutch banks, insurance companies, pension funds, and government departments use TMap partly or wholly. Increasing numbers of small and medium-sized enterprises (SMEs) have adopted TMap and new market segments have been penetrated, such as consumer electronics, telecommunications, and logistics. The TMap book (in Dutch) proved to be a best seller; international interest and awareness resulted in the release of an English version (Pol *et al.*, 1998).

B.1 Testing as a process

For all types of testing the main activities are planning, preparation, and execution. An important part of the effort is spent in planning and preparation. As a rule of thumb the following distribution of effort can be used: 20% planning, 40% preparation and finally 'only' 40% during test execution. Without going into great detail, this means that during the creation of the functional specification a master test plan is established. The master test plan describes who performs which type of testing and when. Ideally this master test plan covers all types of tests, from unit testing to acceptance testing. However, sometimes the scope is limited to only high-level testing (system and acceptance testing) or only low-level testing (unit and integration testing). Since these types of test plans affect several disciplines, the various objectives, tasks, responsibilities, and deliverables have to be described accurately.

In larger projects an assignment with respect to the creation and subsequent coordination of the execution of such a test plan is often the responsibility of the manager of an independent (high-level) test team. On the basis of an agreed master test plan, more detailed test plans are made, mostly one for low-level testing, one for system testing, and one for acceptance testing (Figure B.2). These separate test plans are the responsibility of the various parties involved in the testing process.

After defining the test plans, in parallel with specification, design, and coding activities, the test cases and test infrastructure can be developed. After delivery of the test object, the test cases will be executed. Structured testing introduces, in addition to system design, a second design process: test design. It would appear to be an expensive activity, but with careful

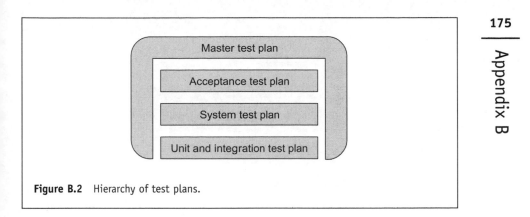

Figure B.2   Hierarchy of test plans.

planning, thorough risk assessment, a well-founded testing strategy, and an early start, costs are reduced considerably. Practice shows that the design of test cases, including the review of the requirements specification, reveals a large number of defects, thus paying back the costs before the first tests have even been executed. It is known that rework effort on defects increases exponentially per development phase (Boehm, 1979).

B.2 Test life cycle

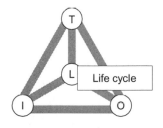

The testing activities can be organized by means of a life-cycle model that operates in parallel with the life-cycle models for system development. In the TMap life-cycle model the three main testing activities are divided into five phases. In addition to the planning and control, preparation, specification, and test execution phases, a completion phase has been defined to finish the testing process in a structured way and to preserve the testware for the first or next maintenance release.

The TMap life-cycle model is a generic model (Figure B.3). It is, in principle, applicable to all types of testing. For low-level tests it contains too many activities. Only in highly critical circumstances will all activities be applicable. It is to up to the test manager to select the required elements from the possibilities offered by TMap (Figure B.4). Within the hierarchy of the test plans several tailored TMap models will be operational for different types of tests. In the rest of this appendix the outline of the generic model is described. This also applies to the terminology; 'specification'(s) should be interpreted as requirements specification *and* as technical design.

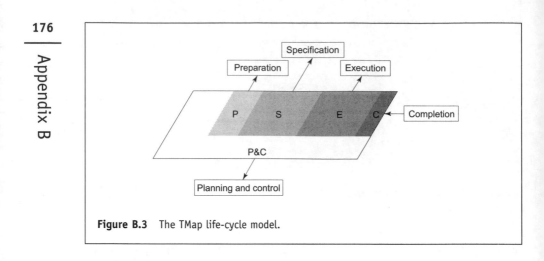

Figure B.3 The TMap life-cycle model.

B.2.1 The planning and control phase

The planning and control phase starts during the specification of the functional requirements. The planning phase provides the basis for a manageable and high-quality testing process. No matter how hard, at an

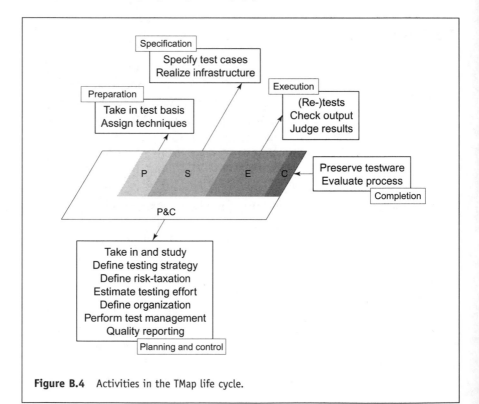

Figure B.4 Activities in the TMap life cycle.

early stage during system development all those things that make the testing process difficult to manage and control have to be discussed. For example, the actual value of the development planning, the expected quality of the test object, the organization of the various tasks, and the availability of staff, infrastructure, and time. The planning phase is the most important testing phase; however, it is often underestimated.

After the test assignment has been agreed, which is absolutely necessary, the test team starts by studying the specifications, the functionality, and the (project) organization. It is impossible to test a software product completely. In theory, 100% coverage is possible, but no organization has the time and money to achieve it, which is why the testing strategy is determined by means of risk assessment: which parts of the system will get more attention during testing and which less, and so on, depending on the risks involved. Defining the test strategy is basically a communication process with all parties involved, trying to define the most important parts of the software product. The aim is to have the most feasible coverage of the right parts of the software product. In addition, the first steps are taken toward structuring the testing organization and defining the test infrastructure. All these activities are performed at the beginning of the testing process.

The other activities of the planning and control phase are carried out throughout the entire testing process with the objective of managing the progress of testing with regard to the time and resources used. If necessary, detailed plans are drawn up for each phase during the testing process. In accordance with the test plan, reporting is done on the progress of testing and on the quality of the test object. The most important deliverable of testing is the quality report, which also describes the accompanying risks. Right from the start of the testing process, testers are developing a view of the quality. It is important that during all phases of the testing process quality indicators are established. Periodically, and when asked ad hoc, management receives a quality report on the status of the test object. This is done continuously, not only at the end of the process. It is necessary that the test team provide well-structured management information. One cannot just say just before the end of the testing process: 'No, you cannot go to production, I have not finished testing yet'! No manager wants these types of comments. A manager wants to know the risks and what actions should be taken. It is, for example, possible to decide to continue testing, partly go into production, or to keep the old system operational in parallel with the new one (shadowing).

B.2.2 The preparation phase

The preparation phase starts as soon as possible after the test plan has been drawn up and agreed. The first activity during this phase is the training of test staff. Once the first version of the specifications is ready, and has an 'adequate' level of quality (for example, most imperfections have been removed), the actual preparation activities can start. It is most important that there is a stable version of the specifications. The specifications are the starting point for both testers and developers. After the establishment of the first version, the specifications can only be changed by way of formal change control. In many cases establishing the first real version takes a long time. The aim is 100% accurate specifications, but this, unfortunately, cannot be achieved. The temptation to start is strong but should be discouraged. Often test design, technical design, and coding activities started prematurely have to be done again. That is frustrating for all parties involved and very expensive.

The preparation phase starts with the detailed study of the specifications and other documentation that serve as a starting point for testing. Insight is acquired into the testability of the specifications by reviewing. During the review, aspects such as the use of standard notations, understandability, and recognizability are important. Using the results of the review, the quality of the test basis, for example the specifications, can be increased. After the study, and with the cooperation of the developers, the test basis will be divided into subsystems that can be independently delivered and tested. Subsequently the test techniques are allocated to each of these test units and a plan is made for the next test phase and its activities.

B.2.3 The specification phase

During the specification phase the test cases are specified and the accompanying test infrastructure realized. The creation of test cases is carried out in two phases, the logical and the physical test design. Once the test basis is available, the logical test cases are specified (test specification). A test case consists of a description of the input, the process to be executed, and a prediction of the expected output, for example results. Later, when more information is available about the technical implementation, the logical test cases are translated into physical test cases (test scripts). During this process the initial content of the test database is also defined. In parallel with the test design, the test infrastructure (the hardware and software environment, and so on) is set up.

B.2.4 The execution phase

The execution phase starts when the first testable components of the software product are available. Agreements have been made with the development teams during previous phases about the delivery schedule and the infrastructure to be used. First, the delivered parts of the software product are checked for completeness and installed in the test environment. Then a test is carried out to establish whether the application environment and technical infrastructure can run without immediate failures. To be able to start the actual tests, the initial test database has to be set up; this is a very important and accurate activity and should be done by using the actual software functions as much as possible. Thus testing has really already started.

When (parts of) the software product, the infrastructure, and the test database are available, the first so-called pretests are executed to check whether the main functions of the object can be tested. The pretests provide an answer to the question: Is the quality of the test object such that it can efficiently and effectively be tested using the prepared test cases? As soon as the pretests have been completed successfully, test execution can start using the test scripts. The execution takes place on the basis of the agreed test strategy. The difference between the actual test result and the expected result can indicate a software product defect, but can also indicate a defect in the specification, a defect in the test infrastructure, or an invalid test case. The cause of the observed difference will be further investigated during the checking and judging activities. As soon as rework has been completed, the tests are executed again.

During the entire test execution phase one should allow for quick and reliable quality reporting. Management will expect to be informed about the risks they must consider. They want to know, for example: What percentage of the product has been tested? What remains to be done? How many defects have been found? What are the trends? Can testing be finished?

B.2.5 The completion phase

When test execution has finished, there are still some important activities to be done. These activities are generally carried out in a less structured way, or even forgotten. The final test execution activities often take place under high pressure. This will mean that concessions to the control procedures are made. The test scene is often chaotic at the time testing 'ends' and the decision is made to go into production. An additional problem that often arises is the phenomenon that during production new defects are found by the users and these must be solved and tested without delay. As a result the completion activities will often get low priority; no time and effort are scheduled, and the testware is not adequately preserved and therefore cannot be reused during the first or next maintenance test.

During the completion phase a selection is made with respect to the large amount of testware, for example test cases, test results, and descriptions of the test infrastructure and the tools used. This has to be done from the perspective of required product changes; the related maintenance tests will only need to be adjusted and no completely new test scripts will have to be designed. During the testing process an effort is made to keep the test cases consistent with the specifications and the software product. When this is carried out successfully, one can truly speak of so-called regressive testware. Keeping consistency between testware, specifications, and the actual software product is an important objective during maintenance.

During the completion phase the testing process is evaluated. The statistics gathered and intermediate reports are combined with the results of the final report. Both the testing process and the quality of the product are evaluated. After the evaluation, the preservation of the testware, and the presentation of the final evaluation report, management will be able to discharge the test team.

B.3 Techniques

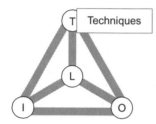

TMap is supported by a large number of testing techniques. These techniques provide test staff with a well-founded and similar way of working and management (and auditors) with the possibility of tracking the testing process with respect to the contents. Throughout the TMap life-cycle model the tester is directed towards the techniques that can be used. Figure B.5 shows the testing techniques available within TMap.

Some of the (groups of) testing techniques identified are briefly described in the following sections.

B.3.1 Defining testing strategy

The definition of the test strategy takes place during the planning phase of the testing process. During this phase the basis is laid for a manageable and high-quality testing process. Defining the test strategy is a mechanism for test management to communicate with the customer, users, developers, and other parties involved about the organization and strategic choices of the testing process. The test strategy defines what is going to be tested and how thoroughly it is going to be tested. Choices have to be made, since it is impossible to test a software product completely; 100% coverage of all functionality and quality characteristics is perhaps possible in theory, but no organization has the time and money to do it. A risk analysis will be the

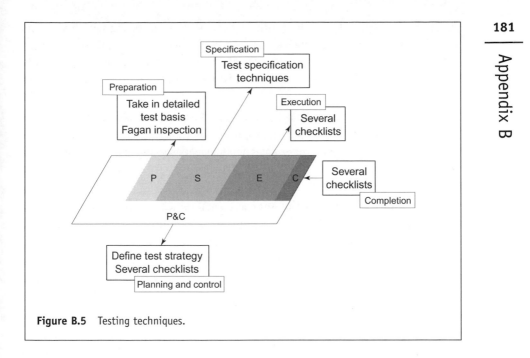

Figure B.5 Testing techniques.

starting point for a well-defined test strategy. The test strategy is further refined and determined via a process of communication by all parties involved, trying to define the most important parts and quality characteristics of the software product. The aim is to have the most feasible coverage of the right parts and quality characteristics of the software product.

B.3.2 Test specification techniques

Using the specifications **test cases** must be determined. An elementary test case consists of a specification of the starting situation, the changing process, and a prediction of the expected result (Figure B.6).

A test case can aim at testing one or more quality characteristics of one or more features of the software product. *Test specification techniques* are available to deduce the test cases from the specifications. The individual test

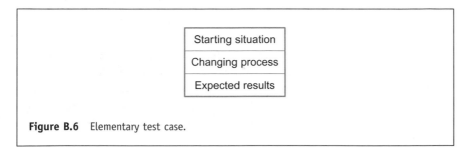

Figure B.6 Elementary test case.

cases are subsequently grouped into test scripts that prescribe which starting situation and which sequence of actions and checks are applicable during the execution of the test. The collection of test scripts is combined into an overall test procedure that also describes the relationship with the required test infrastructure.

A test specification technique is a standardized way to derive test cases from the development documentation, for example requirements specification or technical design.

For testing the various quality characteristics different specification techniques are available. The way a technique is applied depends on the way the specifications are structured. Taking the testing strategy and the structure of the development documentation as a starting point, the appropriate test specification techniques are selected and tailored during the preparation phase.

B.3.3 Checklists

TMap offers a large number and variety of checklists. For the planning and control and preparation phases, the checklists available can be used for support during the study and review, the definition of constraints and starting points, the risk analysis, and the definition of the test facilities and infrastructure. Quality characteristic checklists are available to support the test execution phase, especially with respect to static tests. Evaluation checklists support the final reporting and completion activities.

B.4 Infrastructure and tools

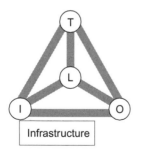

Infrastructure

The infrastructure for testing includes all facilities and resources needed for structured testing. A distinction can be made regarding the test infrastructure between test environment, test tools, and office environment. Choosing an infrastructure for testing is often not an option. A test environment is already available, there are test tools, and an office environment for testing exists. The choice is then limited to change requests regarding the existing infrastructure. In addition, the infrastructure strongly depends on the type of hardware platform and the organization. Because of these issues TMap is limited to the generic level and can only offer some supporting ideas.

B.4.1 Testing environment

Traditionally three types of test environment are available: the laboratory environment for low-level tests, the (more) controllable system test environment, and the 'as-if-production' environment for acceptance testing. Owing, often, to efficiency considerations, the particular circumstance of testers having their 'own' environment is being abandoned. It is much more efficient to determine the testing environment needed on the basis of the type of test that has to be carried out.

Low-level tests require a completely different test environment from, for example, production acceptance tests (PAT). However, sometimes parts of a production acceptance test do not have to be performed in an 'as-if-production' environment. Which quality characteristics are tested? Are formal procedures and/or actual database sizes necessary? Or is having the possibility of doing a quick adjustment to the test object more important for the progress of the testing process? These types of questions have to be answered at an early stage of the testing process, especially since it takes time to prepare the facilities and environment. The computer centers that usually offer these types of facilities to testers have to be informed of the requirements accurately and on time. To prevent disappointment, it is strongly recommended (or even necessary) to get assistance from computer center staff during the definition of these requirements.

B.4.2 Test tools

The development of test tools has matured over the past years. The application and variety have increased enormously. Test tools can be subdivided according to the support they provide to the TMap life-cycle activities. The most important support is currently being provided to the planning and control phase and test execution phase. For *planning* and *progress tracking* the same tools can be used as in every other process, for example planning packages, spreadsheets, and risk-analysis packages. For the *execution* and *judgment* of tests a multitude of tools are used, for example tools that can 'capture' a test session and automatically play it back afterwards (Capture & Playback), tools that automatically compare test results with the results of a preceding test session (comparator), and so on.

For the *remaining phases* tools are available which, for example, support the loading and control of test databases, configuration management, the registration of test defects, and the gathering and presentation of statistics and performance indicators.

Office environment

The testing process, from planning to completion, demands a suitable office environment. This may seem self-evident; however, practice shows that testers do not have desks and PCs available on time, or they have to share them with their colleagues.

B.5 Organization

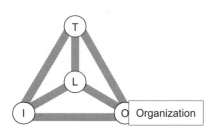

Nearly every testing process with insufficient organization will end in failure. The involvement of many different disciplines (Figure B.7), the unpredictability of the process, the complex control activities, a lack of experience, and the time pressures put severe demands on the testing organizing and the various control activities.

A testing organization is the representation of the relationships between test functions, test facilities, and testing activities aimed at performing a structured test (Thierry, 1973).

The following aspects need attention in the context of organizing structured testing:

- the operational testing process
- the structural testing organization
- test management
- staffing and education
- structuring of the testing process.

B.5.1 The operational testing process

On a departmental or project level where the actual testing processes take place, it is important to set up a flexible, but at the same time stable, organization. This calls for experience, tact, patience, and the timing skills of (test) management. The establishment of testing functions and especially control resources is an ongoing process of making choices between progress and quality. Getting staff or acquiring tools too early or too late are classical problem areas in the testing process.

An operational testing organization consists of a variety of functions. Depending on the type of test and the size of the test object, these functions are performed by one or more persons. Sometimes a test team consists of

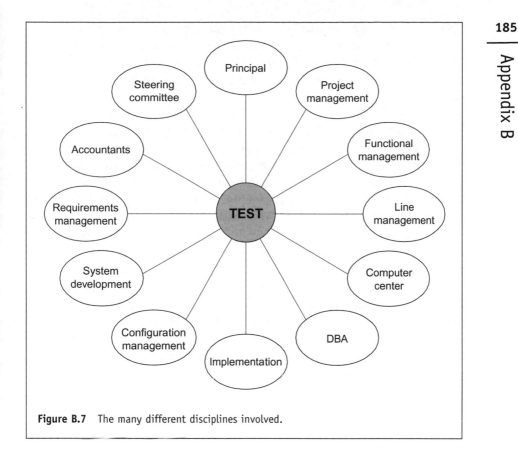

Figure B.7 The many different disciplines involved.

one part-time employee; in large projects a (high-level) test team may involve 20 or more employees. The most important test functions are: testers, test management, and test control. TMap recommends carrying out high-level tests in a project organization (test team). It is important to get the right combination of expertise in an operational testing organization:

- knowledge and skills in the area of testing;
- functional knowledge with respect to the test object (software product);
- knowledge and experience of test management and control;
- knowledge and experience in the area of infrastructure and tools.

B.5.2 The structural testing organization

The organization and control of the structural testing depend on a large number of items, such as the maturity level and the size of the organization.

Of course the IT dependency of an organization is also a great influence; is it possible to allow an error to occur or will even a minor incident reach the front page of the *Wall Street Journal*? How important is time-to-market? Do human lives depend on the software product or are 'only' personal careers damaged?

The test functions can be subdivided into those related to providing adequate conditions and those related to providing operational functions. Functions related to providing conditions are, for example, test regulation, coordination of the testing processes, test management, method support, and technical support. In large organizations in which the software products are closely related to the primary processes, as in banking and insurance companies and some government agencies, these types of test functions are often established at several levels of the structural organization. The operational tasks, for example test execution, are then carried out at a project level. In other organizations a mixture exists or only the separation between test regulation and test execution is present. Often regulation and auditing functions are positioned in a Quality Assurance and/or Methods & Techniques department. In other cases a special testing office or a test service department is operational. Sometimes something is only organized at departmental or project level. In short, as already stated: *A universal type of organization does not exist for testing.*

B.5.3 Test management and control

Management, taken from *managing*, basically means keeping under control. This sentence reflects the test management and control function. One of the typical problems of a testing process is that everything, even the environment, is changing all the time. These changes have to be controlled so as to give a solid quality indication with respect to the test object. Within the testing processes three management and control aspects can be distinguished:

- management and control of the testing process;
- management and control of the testing infrastructure;
- management and control of the test deliverables.

Depending on the type of organization, management is carried out completely or partially at the operational level or at the level of the structural organization. Some management tasks, like management of the test object and/or test database, are essentially arranged outside of the testing process. Within the management of the testing process, it is of greater importance to have the right attitude than to follow a strict set of rules. Management can be looked upon as an environmental control of the testing process. One does not allow a test database or defect to lie around; that is just *not done*!

B.5.4 Staffing and education

Testing has evolved in the past years into a true profession. The growing need for solid tests and the related developments in the area of testing require specialist knowledge and skills and the accompanying education. This does not mean that testing is restricted to specialized testers. A user, a product manager, or a developer can or must perform testing in addition to his or her primary tasks. A test team consists of a large variety of disciplines which, some part-time, contribute their specific expertise. Adequate participation of testing specialists is of course essential, both in the area of test management and in the area of testing techniques. Test staffing requires a lot of (test) management attention.

The function requirements demand that testers have a great variety of knowledge and skills. An education program for test staff naturally has to contain test-specific components such as test management and testing techniques. In addition, it also has to provide a general knowledge of quality assurance and system development. Social skills should also be covered. There are a variety of options, but as for many other educational programs, a combination of theory and practical application is strongly recommended. The best results are obtained by means of a brief theoretical introduction followed by adequate on-the-job training.

Test tools

C.1 Categories of test tools

For each test phase various categories of test tools can be distinguished. Without being exhaustive an overview is given of categories of tools which can support the test process.

C.1.1 Planning and control tools

- **Planning** To support planning in large test processes, a tool is indispensable. Before a plan can be consigned to a progress-monitoring package, it must be worked out completely with respect to the duration of the activities, the start and (if necessary) end dates, and the resources allocated. In general, planning packages provide 'What if' predictions and they are able to generate Gantt charts as well as network planning. An important aspect in the selection of planning packages is the facility to provide management information, for example resource and cost overviews. The functionality of a planning package is often integrated with the functionality of a progress-monitoring package.

- **Progress monitoring** For controlling progress in large processes a tool is almost indispensable. Progress-monitoring packages should offer the functionality to:
  - obtain knowledge about the progress made related to budget, time, and products, and also to provide reports concerning these issues;
  - make accurate predictions of the time and resources still needed to complete the test process.

A progress-monitoring package is a tool for measuring and managing the project's progress. To do this, the activities to be carried out are broken down into basically independent tasks. Planned hours, worked hours, and hours remaining are recorded for each task; reporting is then possible on the basis of this data. The functionality of a progress-monitoring package is often integrated with the functionality of a planning package.

- **Configuration management** During the test process all kinds of products are created which together form the testware. It is of great importance that the products are managed adequately during a test process. After creation and a quality check, the products (for example test cases, documentation) must be finalized and agreed. They become a configuration item. The management of these configuration items and the changes made to them can be supported by a configuration management tool. Such a tool supports the management of the versions of objects (and so also of the testware) created over time.

- **Defect administration** During a test process a large number of defects are often found. During the preparation and specification phases, most of the defects relate to the test basis; during the execution phase they relate mainly to the test object. The number of defects can, depending on, among other things, the size and complexity of the test object, run into hundreds and sometimes even thousands. Defect management is therefore a complex and in many cases extensive activity. To support this activity tools are available for registering defects and monitoring the life cycle of the defects ('problem tracking'). Some tools also provide reporting and statistical functionality, which can be used in formulating reports concerning quality.

- **Test management** Such tools are in fact a collection of the already mentioned categories of test tools, in which much emphasis is laid on the integration of these tools. The tool is used to steer the test process, from the making of the test plan up to the reporting of the results.

C.1.2 Preparation and specification

- **CASE tool analyzer** If the test basis is defined in a CASE tool, such tools can do several evaluations regarding the completeness and consistency of the test basis. For example, they can provide scripts that check whether attribute names that are no longer current are still used somewhere.

- **Test specification** Formal test specification techniques can also be applied or supported by a computer. A precondition is that the functional documentation should be recorded in a formal notation. The danger of such far-reaching automation is that errors of interpretation already made are not found. On the other hand, consistency errors in the pseudo code are easily found.

C.1.3 Execution and analysis tools

- **Capture & Playback**   These tools capture test input (data and actions) and are able to perform an automatic replay, so that the test can easily be repeated at a later time. Usually these kinds of tools provide facilities to create test input and to alter already saved input. In general, Capture & Playback tools are used in combination with comparators to enable analysis of the test results.

  Because Capture & Playback tools require a certain level of stability of the test basis and the test object in order to automatically perform the test quickly and easily each time, a Capture & Playback tool is extremely suitable for regression testing (when the system is supposed to be stable).

- **Load & Stress**   These are tools that can place a load on an application by simulating (large numbers of) users, with the aim of testing whether the system keeps functioning correctly and quickly under heavy loads.

- **Test coverage**   This kind of test tool delivers information about the extent to which the IT system is tested/covered by the executed tests. Test coverage tools measure how the test process covers the structure of the software. The measurements can be carried out at a module level or at a subsystem level. However, a structural test coverage of 100% (statement coverage) does not guarantee that testing was complete!

- **Simulators**   Such a tool simulates the operation of the environment of the (part of the) system to be tested. A simulator is used to test software which is too expensive, dangerous, or even impossible to test in the real environment, for example testing the control software of an airplane, a nuclear reactor, or a chemical control process. The simulator delivers input to the test object, and the test object then treats the input concerned as if it were real input. The output of the test object is redirected by the simulator before the real actions are performed. A simulator can be seen as a special kind of test driver that emulates the environment of the test object.

- **Test data generator**   Such a tool helps in building physical test data-bases. By using test data generators, among other things, the database can be filled randomly using the file and/or database specification. In this way a large test database can be created in a relatively short time for use in, for example, a real-life test.

- **Drivers** A test driver, also called a test harness, makes it possible to execute a number of consecutive tests automatically. The test driver steers the test. The test input is delivered in sequence to the test object and the output is either saved for later comparison or compared to the expected output by a comparator.

- **Compiler** A compiler can perform many evaluations during compiling, such as detection of non-initialized variables, unused code, endless loops, and so on. In practice, the features of compilers are often not fully used.

- **Comparator** Often these tools are integrated in the Capture & Playback tools, but also very simple file compare utilities or even the revision functionality of a word processor can be used.

- **Static analyzer** There are packages that use software as input and perform all kinds of static analyses and evaluations. The difficulty with these tools is that they are often dependent on the development environment (hardware, software, and so on). This is a static analysis, as opposed to dynamic testing where the software is actually running as it is tested. This means that it needs no input data and no output prediction and that the software does not generate output. Also, a tool can be developed which evaluates the software on (a part of) the norms and standards.

EXAMPLE C.1

One of the test aspects of a test project is evaluating the quality characteristic 'Maintainability.' To do this, the source code is checked to see that it meets the programming standards. The developer indicates that this test is superfluous, because all programmers receive a copy of the standards and do their own evaluation by means of a checklist.

When a calculation is done to see how much time it would take the test team to do these evaluations, it turns out to be considerable. If necessary, spot-checks can be done, but a disadvantage is their incompleteness. A tester remarks that it would not require much work to make a program that inspects other programs for use of (a part of) the standards. The program is made and is immediately used to evaluate the first delivery from a developer. A 100% rejection 'score' is the result; not a single delivered source meets the standards. Soon it is decided to give the program to the developers as well, because otherwise the percentage of rejections will be unacceptably high. The result is that the sources delivered in future fully comply with the standards (that is, those checked by the program!). The disadvantage is of course that the program does not check all standards, but a relatively small effort ensures that the sources meet at least a substantial part of the standards.

- **Query languages** A query language enables the tester to retrieve information about the contents of test databases by means of short concise commands. A query language is pre-eminently a tool to investigate a potential defect further. Some query languages also provide data manipulation, thus being of assistance in maintaining the starting test database.

- **Debugger** Strictly speaking, a debugger is not a tool for testing. By means of a debugger, specific errors, which are hard to find, can be traced and then solved. Debugger tools enable developers to view, depending on the tool, program logic and data at a source and/or object level.

- **Monitor** To gain insight into aspects such as memory, CPU, and network usage and time-behavior, monitoring tools can be used during the test process. All kinds of data regarding the usage of resources are measured and recorded. The measuring data is then presented to the test team by means of a report. Setting up these tools is usually a complex matter. Often monitoring tools are already present in the computer department for monitoring the operational system environment. It is probable that the facilities of these monitoring tools can be used in the test environment.

C.2 Capture & Playback tools

Because there is a fairly large chance of an implementation failure with Capture & Playback tools, some critical factors are explained here.

The problem in using (especially) a Capture & Playback tool is that a certain stability (of the application) is required to automate these tests. Inherent in testing, however, is the fact that the application is not stable. A keyword in a well-automated test is good **maintainability**. It should be possible to adjust an automated test with relatively little effort for a changed application. To do this, attention must be paid to a number of issues:

- **Earlier and more thinking** Building automated test scripts requires earlier and more thinking. It is not enough to push the Capture button so that all activities are captured. Good thinking must be done about strategy, modularity, and so on. This should start early, to prevent it having to be done during test execution, which causes delay.

- **Strategy** Most Capture & Playback tools can test many things, from screen colors to even the hidden properties of a button. The tendency is to maximize test automation, but the drawback is that much test work leads to much investigating, and an increase in the maintenance of test scripts.

Which tests can be automated? A regression test is an obvious choice, whereas a detailed sub-test that causes at most one or two retests is not. Automation can be started from the first test execution, or when the application is more stable.

- **Modularity** The basic principles of modular programming also apply to automated tests. Each group of consecutive actions that must be executed repeatedly (for example, moving to a certain function) can best be saved as a separate module; tests that have to execute these activity groupings call this module. When something changes in the group of activities (for example, as a result of another menu structure), only one module has to be changed.

- **Starting situation** At capture time there should be a clear starting situation, involving the contents of the database, the position in the application (which window is active), and the number of running programs. Exactly the same starting situation must exist at playback time, otherwise the results will be unpredictable.

- **Error handling** Usually series of automated test cases will be executed consecutively, often unattended. When a test case goes wrong, with the result that other test cases can no longer be executed, this is very disrupting. Error handling means that the test cases are made more 'robust,' decreasing the chance of mutual disruption. For example, for each series of test cases the database is reloaded, or each test case begins with a number of keyboard entries (for example, ESC) which cause the application to start in the main menu.

  How much effort is put into error handling depends on the risks. If a short test lead time is very important, then more effort must be put into it.

- **Documentation** For an average test some hundreds of automated test cases will soon exist. To increase maintainability, attention must be given to instructions for commenting the scripts, version management, naming conventions, authorization rules (who can edit which scripts), and so on.

- **Traceability** Related to documentation, it is also important that the relationship with the test cases, and therefore with the test basis, is sustained. On the one hand, it can be easily established which part of the test basis is involved when a certain automated test case does not react according to expectations. On the other hand, it must be clear which test cases must be adjusted when the test basis is changed.

- **Tools expertise** Although a number of suppliers say that Capture & Playback tools are suited for end users, this is mainly valid if the tools are only used to log test actions. When an automated test must be built, a tools expert is needed. Programming in the language of the tool is almost always necessary.

- **Check captured scripts** When an automated test case falsely reports during playback that a result is not according to expectations, this is disrupting. The opposite case, saying nothing when the result does deviate from expectations, can have very serious consequences!

  In fact this means that captured test cases must be tested! This can be done by adjusting the expectations incorrectly and then playing back the test case: the error must be reported. Although this double testing is not always necessary, the above-mentioned risks should be handled consciously.

  In any case, a test case captured for the first time should be played back immediately, to check that the capturing went well. This is even more important if programming is used to automate the test.

- **Unrecognized objects** When certain screen objects are not recognized by the tool, automated testing becomes difficult, even impossible. It is true that bitmap snapshots can always be taken, but their maintainability is nil. By the way, in the selection of the tool in particular, attention must be given to the presence of this problem.

- **Test script pollution** Capturing a test case is different from executing a test manually. Because all kinds of mistakes, such as Backspace, wrong menu choices, and so on, are captured directly, there can be a negative influence on maintainability. Therefore accurate capturing is important, but also much more time-consuming.

- **Too much confidence** When the final aim, a fully automated test, is achieved, we cannot just sit back and relax. What is lacking is human intuition and the ability to take a sidestep. The automated test is as 'clever' as the tester who defined it in the past. That is why a warning must be given against having 'too much confidence' in the automated test; there must always be room left for manual test execution.

- **Keeping up with developments** What goes for unrecognized objects also goes here. New versions of development environments can in theory cause automated tests to stop working. The tool suppliers, however, recognize this problem, and usually have agreements with the suppliers of development environments to provide them with beta versions at an early stage.

- **Tricky analysis** Analyzing a test that went wrong can be very time-consuming and the test case will often be repeated manually. The cause can even be invisible! When, for example, internal naming in an application changes, this is not visible from the outside, but the automated test can lose track completely.

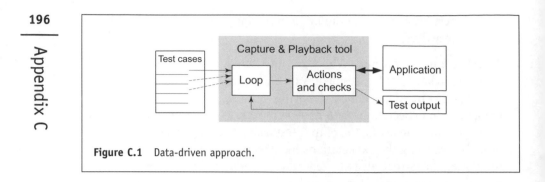

Figure C.1 Data-driven approach.

A separate technique to solve the maintenance problem of automated test scripts is the data-driven test approach (Figure C.1). In this approach, test control (navigating through the application) is separated from the test data. The test data is placed, together with reference to the control to be executed (for example, 'add person') in a separate file. So this file contains lines such as 'add person; Smith; J.; 07-06-1963; 12 Church Road; Maintown'. The automated test script reads the file line by line, reads the reference to the appropriate control, and performs that control, entering data from the file in places where test input is required. When changes in the application are made, only a few modules in the test suite have to be adjusted. This also enables extra test cases to be added easily and quickly, thus greatly reducing the maintenance effort.

Below is an example of the difference between 'normal' Capture & Playback scripts and data-driven scripts for 30 test cases, to test the function 'Order entry.'

EXAMPLE C.2

'Pure' Capture & Playback:

- Script Order entry 1
- Script Order entry 2
- Script Order entry...
- Script Order entry 30

When a change is made in the function, for example 'Exit' with F10 instead of F12, all 30 scripts have to be changed.

Data-driven:

- Script Order entry (variable input)
- File containing:
  'Enter order', test data 1
  'Enter order', test data...
  'Enter order', test data 30

- Script that reads the file, calls the script 'Order entry' and inserts the test data.

When a change is made in the function, for example 'Exit' with F10 instead of F12, only the script 'Order entry' has to be changed.

IQUIP has developed the approach TAKT (Testing, Automation, Knowledge, Tools), which converts the manual test process into an automated test process for faster and better testing. Within this approach, among other things, the data-driven principle described above is used. TAKT is based on Pol *et al.* (1995), Andersen Consulting (1995), Feurster *et al.* (1998), Burghouts (1995) and Kaner (1997).

Glossary

Acceptance test   A test, executed by the user(s) and manager(s) in an environment simulating the operational environment to the greatest possible extent, that should demonstrate that the developed system meets the functional and quality requirements.

Black-box test techniques   Test specification techniques that derive test cases from the externally visible properties of an object, without having knowledge of the internal structure of this object.

CASE   Computer Aided Software Engineering.

CAST   Computer Aided Software Testing.

Compatibility   The extent to which the manual procedures are compatible with the IT system and the practicability of these manual procedures for the organization.

Correctness   The extent to which the system processes the presented input and changes correctly, according to the specification, into consistent data collections.

Coverage   The ratio between that which can be tested (possible number of test aims) and that which is in fact tested. Often used in relation to program code ('with the available test cases X% statement coverage or condition coverage is reached') but also possible in relation to the functional specifications (paths, conditions, or interfaces).

Defect   The differences found between the expectations and the actual results.

Dynamic testing   Testing, based on specific test cases, by execution of the test object or running programs.

Evaluation   The evaluation and inspection of the various intermediate products and/or processes in the system development cycle. Within the scope of this book only the evaluation of the intermediate products is described.

Function point analysis   Function point analysis (FPA) is a method enabling a technology-independent measurement of the size of the functionality provided by an automated system and the use of this measurement as a basis for productivity measurement, an estimate of the means required, and project management.

Functionality   The extent to which a set of functions and their specified properties exists that satisfies the stated or implied needs.

High-level tests   These tests involve testing whole, complete products (Kit, 1995). As their focus is often the externally visible properties of an object, high-level tests commonly use black-box techniques. Well-known high-level tests are the system and acceptance tests.

Inspection of test basis   Evaluation of the testability of the test basis (for instance, requirements or functional specifications).

Integration test   A test, executed by the developer in a laboratory environment, that should demonstrate that a logical series of programs meets the requirements set in the design specifications.

Low-level tests   These test levels involve testing the separate components, for instance programs, of a system, individually or in combination (Kit, 1995). As the low-level tests require good knowledge of the internal structure of the software, mainly white-box testing techniques are applicable. The tests are almost exclusively executed by developers. Well-known low-level tests are the unit and integration tests.

Maintainability   The ease with which specified modifications to the IT system can be made. Kinds of modifications are adaptation to new user requirements, changes to the external environment, or the correction of defects.

Online   Function mode of an IT system in which the IT system immediately processes the commands and directly shows the answer (output) on the screen (or elsewhere).

Portability   The diversity of the hardware and software platform on which the IT system can run, and the ease with which the system can be ported from one environment to another.

Pretest Testing the delivered product in such a way that it can be determined whether or not it is useful to execute a test with respect to the product.

Quality The totality of features and characteristics of a product or service that bear on its ability to satisfy stated or implied needs (ISO 8402).

Quality assurance All planned and systematic actions necessary to provide adequate confidence that a product or service will satisfy given requirements for quality (ISO 8402).

Quality characteristic Property of an IT system. Examples of quality characteristics are security, time-behavior, usability (ISO 9126).

Regression test Regression is the phenomenon that the quality of a system decreases as a result of individual adjustments. The aim of a regression test is to check that all parts of a system still function correctly after a change has been made.

Security Attributes of software that bear on its ability to prevent unauthorized access, whether accidental or deliberate, to programs or data (ISO 9126).

Static testing Testing by inspecting products (such as manuals or source code), without programs being run.

System test A test, executed by the developer in a (properly controlled) laboratory environment, that should demonstrate that the developed system or subsystems meet the requirements set in the functional and quality specifications.

Test action An action in a previously defined start situation which produces a result. A test action is part of a test case.

Test basis All documents from which the requirements of an IT system can be extracted. The documentation on which the test is based. If a document can only be changed through the formal change procedure it is called a fixed test basis.

Test basis defects Missing or incorrect specifications, especially those which are found during the Preparation and Specification phases.

Test case A description of a test to be executed, focused on a specific test aim.

Test infrastructure The environment in which the test is performed, consisting of hardware, system software, test tools, procedures, and so on.

Test level A test level is a group of test activities that are organized and managed together. They can be divided into high-level and low-level tests.

Test object   The IT system (or part of it) which is to be tested.

Test organization   A test organization comprises all of the test functions, facilities, procedures, and activities, including their relationships.

Test plan   In a test plan the general structure and the strategic choices with respect to the test to be executed are formulated. The test plan forms the scope of reference during the execution of the test and also serves as an instrument to communicate with the customer of the test. The test plan is a description of the test project, including a description of the activities and the planning; therefore it is *not* a description of the tests themselves.

Test point   Unit of measurement for the size of the high-level test to be executed.

Test point analysis   Test point analysis (TPA) is a method giving the possibility of performing a technology-independent measurement of the test size of an information system, on the basis of a function point analysis, and of using this measurement as a basis for productivity measurement, an estimate of the required resources, and project management.

Test process   The collection of tools, techniques, and working methods used to perform a test.

Test script   A sequence of related actions and checks, related to test cases, whose sequence of execution is indicated. A description of *how* the testing is done.

Test set   A collection of test cases specifically aimed at one or more quality characteristics and one or more test units.

Test specification technique   A standardized way to extract test cases from output information.

Test team   A group which, led by a test manager, takes on the test activities.

Test technique   A test technique is a collection of actions to produce a test product in a universal manner.

Test unit   A part of the test object (that is, a collection of programs, functions, or processes) that is tested as a whole.

Testability   Attributes of software that bear on the effort needed for validating the modified software (ISO d402).

Testability   The ease and speed with which the functionality and the performance level of the system (after adjustments) can be tested (TPI definition).

Testing Testing is a process of planning, preparation, and measurement aimed at establishing the characteristics of an information system and demonstrating the difference between the actual and the required status.

Testware All test documentation, such as test specifications, test scripts, a description of the test infrastructure, and so on, which is produced during the test process. A requirement is that this test documentation can be reused for maintenance purposes and therefore must be portable and maintainable.

Time-behavior The speed with which the IT system handles interactive and batch transactions.

Unit test A test, executed by the developer in a laboratory environment, that should demonstrate that the program meets the requirements set in the design specifications.

Usability The ease with which an end user can learn to handle the IT system and the ease of use of the IT system for experienced users.

White-box test techniques Test specification techniques that derive test cases from the internal properties of an object, with knowledge of the internal setup of the object.

Bibliography

ANDERSEN CONSULTING (1995). *Technology Discussion on Testing Tools: Establish 'parameterized testing' environment (aka data-driven testing)*

BEIZER B. (1990). *Software Testing Techniques*. International Thomson Computer Press, ISBN 1-850-32880-3

BENDER R. (1996). *SEI/CMM Proposed Software Evaluation and Test KPA*, STAR '96

BOEHM B.W. (1979). *Software Engineering Economics*. Englewood Cliffs NJ: Prentice Hall, Inc.

BOETERS A. and NOORMAN B. (1997). *Kwaliteit op maat* [Quality tailor-made]. Kluwer Bedrijfsinformatie, ISBN 90-267-2579-5

BOREEL M. and FRANKEN P. (1997). *Gevangen tussen verleden en toekomst: legacy-systemen in het informatietijdperk* [Caught between past and future: legacy systems in the information era]. IQUIP, ISBN 9075-414-06-4

BURGHOUTS P. (1995). *CAST: Computer-Aided Software Testing and the Concept of CMG Finance*. Internal unpublished paper [in Dutch]

BURNS T. and STALKER G.M. (1995). *The Management of Innovation*. Oxford University Press, ISBN 0-19-828878-6

BURNSTEIN I., SUWANNASART T. and CARLSON C.R. (1996). *Developing a Testing Maturity Model: Parts I and II*. Illinois Institute of Technology

DEMING W. EDWARDS (1992). *Out of the Crisis*. University of Cambridge, ISBN 0-521-30553-5

EMAM K. El and DROUIN J. (eds) (1998). *Spice: The Theory and Practice of Software Process Improvement and Capability Determination.* IEEE Computer Society, ISBN 0-81867-798-8

ERICSON T., SUBOTIC A., and URSING S. (1996). *Towards a Test Improvement Model.* EuroSTAR '96

GELPERIN D. (1996). *A Testability Maturity Model.* STAR '96

GRADY R.B. and CASWELL D.L. (1987). *Software Metrics: Establishing a Company-Wide Program.* Prentice Hall, ISBN 0-13-821844-7

GRAHAM D., HERZLICH P., and MORELLI C. (1996). *Computer Aided Software Testing, The CAST-report.* Cambridge Market Intelligence Limited, ISBN 1-897977-74-3

HALL T.J. (1995). *The Quality Systems Manual: The Definitive Guide to the ISO 9000 Family and Tickit.* John Wiley & Sons, ISBN 0-471-95588-4

HETZEL W. (1993). *Making Software Measurement Work.* Wiley-QED, ISBN 0-471-56568-7

HORCH J.W. (1996). *Practical Guide to Software Quality Management.* Artech House Publishers, ISBN 0-89006-865-8

HUMPHREY W.S. (1989). *Managing the Software Process.* Addison-Wesley, ISBN 0-201-18095-2

JARVIS A. and CRANDELL V. (1997). *Inroads to Software Quality.* Prentice Hall, ISBN 0-13-238403-5

JURAN J.M. (1988). *Juran's Quality Control Handbook.* McGraw-Hill, ISBN 0-070-33176-6

KANER C. (1997). Improving the maintainability of automated testing suites. *Software QA,* **4**(4)

KANER C., FALK J., and NGUYEN H.Q. (1993). *Testing Computer Software* 2nd edn. International Thomson Computer Press, ISBN 1-85032-847-1

KIT E. (1995). *Software Testing in the Real World.* Addison-Wesley, ISBN 0-201-87756-2

KUVAJA P., SIMILA J., KRZANIK L., BICEGO A., SAUKKONEN S., and KOCH G. (1994). *Software Process Assessment and Improvement: the Bootstrap Approach.* Blackwell

MACFARLANE I.J. and WARDEN R. (1996). *Testing an IT Service for Operational Use.* HMSO Publications Centre, ISBN 0-11-330560-5

McFEELEY B. (1996). *IDEAL*[sm]: *a user's guide for Software Process Improvement.* Software Engineering Institute

MOSLEY D.J. (1993). *The Handbook of MIS Application Software Testing.* Yourdon, ISBN 0-13-907007-9

MYERS G.J. (1979). *The Art of Software Testing*. New York NY: Wiley-Interscience, ISBN 0-471-04328-1

PERRY W.E. and RICE R.W. (1997). *Surviving the Challenges of Software Testing*. Dorset House Publishing, ISBN 0-932633-38-2

POL M., TEUNISSEN R., and VEENENDAAL E. van (1995). *Testen volgens TMap®* [Testing according to TMap]. Tutein Nolthenius, 's-Hertogenbosch, ISBN 90-72194-33-0

POL M., TEUNISSEN R., and VEENENDAAL E. van (1996). *Gestructureerd Testen: een Introductie tot TMap®* [Structured testing: an introduction to TMap]. Tutein Nolthenius, 's-Hertogenbosch, ISBN 90-72194-45-4

POL M. and VEENENDAAL E. van (1998). *Structured Testing of Information Systems: an Introduction to TMap®*. Kluwer Bedrijfsinformatie, ISBN 90-267-2910-3

PULFORD K., KUNTZMANN-COMBELLES A., and SHIRLAW S. (1995). *A Quantitative Approach to Software Management, the ami Handbook*. Addison-Wesley, ISBN 0-201-87746-5

ROBBINS S.P. (1992). *Gedrag in Organisaties* [Behaviour in Organizations]. Prentice Hall/Academic Service, ISBN 90-4261-062-2

SOFTWARE ENGINEERING INSTITUTE, Carnegie Mellon University (1995). *The Capability Maturity Model*. Addison-Wesley, ISBN 0-201-54664-7

THIERRY H. (1973). *Organization and Management* [in Dutch], 6th ed. Stenfert Kroese, Leiden, The Netherlands, ISBN 90-207-0445-1

TRIENEKENS J. and VEENENDAAL E. van (1997). *Software Quality from a Business Perspective*. Kluwer Bedrijfsinformatie, ISBN 90-267-2631-7

Index

IQUIP and Gitek overview

IQUIP

IQUIP was founded in 1986 and is a part of IQUIP Informatica B.V. Its exclusive aim is the area of testing in an IT environment. Employing more than 250 test specialists, it offers services in the area of implementation of structured testing as well as test management and actual test execution. Training and consultancy are also an important part of the services provided.

To continuously provide maximum availability of the test services offered, IQUIP gives much attention to R & D innovations such as Object Orientation, Client/Server infrastructure, Graphical User Interfaces, and ERP packages. The Internet and Multimedia are closely monitored. Besides TPI, IQUIP offers the following products:

- TMap, a methodology for structured testing;
- TSite, an approach enabling factory-wise organization and exploitation of testing;
- TAKT, an approach for effective automated testing.

IQUIP's customers are government institutions, banks, insurance companies, service and trade industries, and industrial enterprises. IQUIP is one of the leading companies in its line of business. It regularly organizes seminars and workshops concerning subjects related to testing. IQUIP is certified according to ISO 9002.

Address:
IQUIP Informatica B.V.
PO Box 263
1110 AG Diemen
The Netherlands

Gitek nv

Gitek nv was founded in 1986. The company is based in Antwerp (Belgium) and, in addition to the realization of IT systems, has also specialized since 1997 in testing software applications.

Gitek nv employs 35 professional software testers and has customers in the public and banking sectors, the telecommunications industry, and utility companies, as well as insurance companies.

Gitek nv provides services which offer comprehensive testing solutions:

- test advice;
- structuring test processes;
- training and coaching in testing;
- test planning and test management;
- test design and test execution.

Address:
Gitek nv
St. Pietersvliet 3
B-2000 Antwerpen
Belgium